MILE MARKERS

A Path for Nurturing Adolescent Faith

2 9 3

DENISE MCKINNEY

ZONDERVAN®

ZONDERVAN.com/
AUTHORTRACKER
follow your favorite authors

**youth
specialties**

YOUTH SPECIALTIES

Mile Markers: A Path for Nurturing Adolescent Faith
Copyright 2009 by Denise McKinney

Youth Specialties resources, 1890 Cordell Ct. Ste. 105, El Cajon, CA 92020 are published by Zondervan, 5300 Patterson Ave. SE, Grand Rapids, MI 49530.

Library of Congress Cataloging-in-Publication Data

McKinney, Denise R. (Denise Roberts)
    Mile markers : a path for nurturing adolescent faith / Denise McKinney.
      p. cm.
    Includes bibliographical references.
    ISBN 978-0-310-29279-1
    1. Teenagers—Religious life. 2. Discipling (Christianity) 3. Church
work with teenagers. I. Title.
BV4531.3.M4197 2009

259'.23—dc22   2009033746

Cover design by Toolbox Studios
Interior design by SharpSeven Design

Printed in the United States of America

---

09 10 11 12 13 14 15 • 20 19 18 17 16 15 14 13 12 11 10 9 8 7 6 5 4 3 2 1

CONTENTS

7   Preface

9   Chapter 1   Welcome to the Adolescent Road Trip

27 Chapter 2   Embracing the Adolescent Road Trip

41 Chapter 3   Marking Their Miles

65 Chapter 4   The Journey Begins Here

85 Chapter 5   First I Am a Traveler, Then a Guide

103 Chapter 6   Stories from the Road

117 Chapter 7   Conversations on the Road

137 Chapter 8   Mileage Reminders and Celebrations

157 Benediction

158 Bibliography

159 Endnotes

ACKNOWLEDGEMENTS

My husband for unswerving support and sacrifice in my ministry and writing.

My kiddos, for showing me how I need to translate lofty and hopeful ideas into the beautiful noise and craziness of daily, hope-filled living.

Four of my dearest friends and mentors – Sherry, Lana, Marilyn, and Sue – you taught me what it looks like for a parent to walk the road of faith with her kids.

All my youth ministry cohorts in Tulsa Metro Worship - not only did you give honest feedback on the book - but you have always encouraged and taught me as we shared the ministry road together.

Writing buddies – Mark, Toni, Scott, Allison – I love swapping stories, ideas, and opinions with you! You always make me think upon better things!

Bill Clark – as a boss and senior pastor, you modeled spiritual leadership that guides and shepherds.

My excellent editor, Michael, whose comments and critique were always very helpful and edifying.

YS Staff for giving me this chance and showing me the ropes in writing a book!

My parents and Jeff and Cindy Mugford – it's your fault that *Mile Markers* even exists!!!!

DEDICATION

Dedicated to my family - Gary, Lanie, and Garrison – the greatest joy in my own spiritual journey is sharing the road with you three!

To my amazing students, their trusting parents, and our devoted volunteer leaders at Redeemer Covenant Church – I cherished every moment and every mile marker we shared together!

PREFACE

I didn't learn about the idea of mile markers from a book or a class. I didn't borrow it from a seminar presentation. I just gave a name to the way a few people lived and led right in front of me on my own adolescent journey. Although I talk about these individuals in this book, you've most likely never met or even heard about them. They're the ones who've given their lives to leading pilgrims down an amazing, yet treacherous, road. They're the voices that said, "I'll take you there," when no one else would. They're the givers who didn't consider the cost but counted it a joy not to let one sojourner remain lost.

The love and example that my parents, Bob and Dee Moore, gave not only to my siblings and me, but also scores of foster children who came and went for almost two decades, is the mile marker where God breathed life into my calling to walk the adolescent road with students and their families. My parents' willingness to stand in the gap for children without a home birthed my desire to give teenagers healing from their past and hope for a future. The reality that they were serving as "substitute" parents motivated me to help other parents not to give up.

The leadership and nurture that my youth pastors, Jeff and Cindy Mugford, consistently modeled and lavished upon my awkward adolescent existence is the mile marker that showed me how to travel that road with young lives caught between the lands of childhood and adulthood. Their ability to see beyond my nerdy veneer helped me to see God's love for me. Their willingness to take a chance with my hopes and dreams caused me to trust more and more of my life to God's purpose. It was step after step after step of walking beside my life that gave me not only a journey to remember, but the desire to keep living it, too.

I hope I can do for others what they did for me.

WELCOME TO THE ADOLESCENT ROAD TRIP

"The LORD your God has blessed you
in all the work of your hands.
He has watched over your journey
through this vast wilderness.
These forty years the LORD your God
has been with you,
and you have not lacked anything."
Deuteronomy 2:7

CHAPTER

1

A DIFFERENT KIND OF GROWING-UP EXPERIENCE

On an otherwise normal day in 1969, my mom and dad were asked to become foster parents to three children in need of a home. They said yes. And for the next 18 years, they said yes to many more children who then lived with my family. Some stayed for just a few days. Others lived with us for years. Many of the foster children who came to live with us were teenagers who struggled not only with the angst and unknowns of growing up, but also the confusion and pain of traveling that adolescent road alone.

People often ask me how this foster-care arrangement affected my childhood. The most powerful impact of this experience was the fact that I lived in a home with parents who demonstrated great love for me through their time, words, and actions, and I did so alongside kids whose spiritual and emotional health had been taken captive on a long and painful journey. My parents often commented that the older these children were when they came to live with us, the harder it was to break through the walls and defenses they'd built up over the years.

Many of them just couldn't believe in a life filled with purpose and meaning. They were unable to envision a place where they belonged. And their inability to see a bright future affected their perspective on the present. What they'd learned about life to that point pretty much led to never-ending detours and dead ends, so they continued their journeys while making bad choices, which reflected their loss of hope for anything better.

But even with their many protective layers, some of these kids began to hope and trust again—especially those who spent a long time with our family. Maybe nightly dinner gatherings with 12 people arguing, teasing, and laughing around the table began to chip away at their armor. Or quite possibly a vacation trip in the mountains strengthened their hope. And then there were the Christmases that bordered on insanity because of all the presents stacked up in the living room. Maybe those were the kinds of moments when these foster children realized they not only lived in our house, but they also belonged in our family. Maybe that's when they caught a glimpse of possibility and promise.

I believe that in those brief, unnoticed moments the few adolescents who were able to live with us long enough to differentiate wholeness from brokenness gained momentum and determination to strive for better lives than the ones they'd been given. And this transformation was a defining part of my own adolescent journey. During these years spent observing young lives fragmented by instability, damaged by abuse and neglect, and vulnerable to self-destruction, God branded my heart for them.

DIFFERENT STORIES, FAMILIAR ROAD

Now fast-forward a few years to find me serving in youth ministry. Memories of the foster kids I grew up with were embedded in each moment of my teaching and leading. Most of the students I worked with seemed to being doing okay on their journey through adolescence, but they had parents who loved them, resources to meet their needs, and tremendous potential for a bright future.

Yet, many other students demonstrated some of the same characteristics I'd seen in the foster children I lived with years before. They appeared to be living two distinctly different lives—one in front of adults and another in front of their peers. They didn't easily trust adults to lead them or give them direction. They were often overwhelmed with frustration, disappointment, and expectations. And surprisingly, many of them seemed to see only a dead end on the horizon. Early on, I struggled to make sense of why their choices and perspectives reflected people who were living without hope when they had so much to hope for.

Trying to Find the Connection

A few years into youth ministry, I began to better understand the rumblings in my soul. From talking with ministry peers, learning from youth culture experts, and taking time to observe the adolescent experience in the world around me, I realized that I'd witnessed something unique by living alongside foster children for so many years.

Cultural norms seem to begin on the fringes of society, and I certainly grew up with kids whose whole lives had been on the fringe. What if the uncommon struggles of foster children 30 years ago were now becoming common to the adolescent experience? What if kids everywhere now struggled to find their way down a new road of adolescence—much like children without a permanent home? What if as a collective group they were all feeling lost, or abandoned, or scared, or anxious on some level? What would I call that?

Dr. Joe Scruggs is a pastor and counselor whom I admire immensely. At the funeral of a dear friend of mine who lost his lifelong battle with depression several years ago, Joe attempted to help a group of more than 1,000 mourners understand how a person who loved God and cared deeply for others could lose hope in his life and in himself. Dr. Scruggs began with a story about a little boy who tearfully brought a broken toy to his parents and described the mangled pieces as "come from together." Without having the word *broken* in his vocabulary, the child described it with the words he did have. In a similar way, my friend's life had come from together. It was a life meant to be whole and healthy, but his thoughts, his confidence, and his hope had unraveled over time because of terrible mental illness.

That analogy perfectly described the plight of adolescence as I'd personally witnessed it with foster kids and my own students. Young lives that were meant to be healthy, happy, and whole had too quickly and too easily come apart. Yet the process of putting all of the pieces back together was long and difficult. And even though one student's struggle could be much deeper than another's, both teenagers were on a long journey of lost and found experiences.

FAMILIAR ROAD, LONGER JOURNEY

When I talk to adults about adolescence being different in the twenty-first century, they typically don't see much difference between their adolescent experiences and those of today's teens. They certainly see the inevitable strains that society can put on adolescents, but they don't see how the weight of the baggage that teenagers carry on this pilgrimage has gradually grown to become an overwhelming burden.

Several years ago, I began a program through Fuller Seminary with an emphasis on youth, family, and culture. In those studies led by Dr. Chap Clark, I gained foundational ideas for understanding the adolescent journey that in many ways informed my own personal and ministry experience. This section offers a glimpse of those lessons and discussions that continue to shape my ministry perspective and application today.

A Season of Questioning

Have you ever noticed how a three-year-old is a fountain of never-ending questions? "What's that?" "Where are we going?" "How?" and "Why? Why? Why?" Preschoolers' brains are wired to take in a baffling amount of information. Adolescence is another age of questioning, but the answers to these questions are more elusive. Even the questions can be difficult to define. I've never seen them posted on a billboard along the highway, and they don't typically show up as a curriculum bullet point in school.

A student might question her own life's direction while reading Homer's *Odyssey* for English class, or she might wonder about her humanity and responsibility during genetic engineering discussions in biology class. Just as likely, though, she'll be wondering about her level of beauty and worth while she's looking in the mirror, comparing a two-dimensional reflection of herself to an edited and altered two-dimensional picture of a model in a magazine. The soccer player who's breaking school scoring records questions her ability just as much as her teammate who sits on the bench for most of the season. And when teenagers feel like they're out there all alone, their questions with no good answers penetrate even more deeply.

So what are the questions we should be listening for? What are teens asking with their expressions, their actions, and—every so often—their words? What uncertainties do all adolescents wrestle with in both the best and worst of circumstances?

- Who am I? This is a question of identity. How do I define myself? What am I made of? What's my history? What's my story? Should I strive to imitate those around me? Why do I have to be so different? What makes me unique?
- Do I matter? This is a question of purpose. What am I supposed to do with my life? Can I make a difference? Am I important to someone? Do my actions mean anything? Does someone need me? Who do I need?
- Do I belong? This is a question of community. Am I alone? Do people care about me and know me? Am I connected to others in a lasting way? Who would I turn to if I needed help?

Teenagers are definitely asking lots of questions, but I've found that I have to pay attention to when the questions pop up. On the best days, I've observed adolescents asking their questions in small groups, on retreats, and during conversations over coffee with friends and mentors. But I've also noticed them searching for answers at weekend keg parties (with a little meth mixed in), through casual sexual encounters, by abusing their own bodies, and by hurting the people around them. Sometimes they ask the questions in alarming ways, and the adults in their lives often struggle to help them find the answers they seek.

It Used to Be a Sprint—Now It's a Marathon

Fifty years ago, this long journey of personal search and discovery took about four to five years. However, in the last 30 years, this questioning process, called individuation, has extended into a cultural phenomenon that can last well beyond a decade.[1] The reason for such a huge shift in the length of adolescent development isn't a neat and tidy explanation. But Chap Clark explains it as something that "begins in biology and ends in culture."[2]

Both the onset of puberty and changes in cultural norms dramatically affect what adolescence looks like today and how kids experience it. In the 1950s, the onset of puberty was typically at the age of 14 to 15. Now it's all too often occurring around ages 11 to 12. So adolescents are facing an upheaval of their physical, emotional, and social realities at least two years earlier, sometimes four.[3] I have to remind myself that if a 12-year-old girl looks more like a senior in high school, then her physical appearance is just the first indicator that her thoughts, desires, abilities, and interests are moving away from a childhood perspective.

When I think about the challenges I faced when I was 14—anxious about my appearance, stressed about making good grades, worried about nuclear war, dreaming of succeeding as a musician, and on a roller coaster of emotions whenever I liked a guy—I can't fathom carrying that burden at a younger age. With so many changes colliding all at once in their lives, teens can feel tremendous anxiety about the people they're becoming in their appearance, their abilities, and their souls.

Austin was a warmhearted, outgoing seventh grader, and all of the students in our church loved to hang out with him. He was not only fun, but also very accepting of others. Yet Austin didn't see himself that way. He was one of four brothers belonging to an incredible family in our church. Although the four siblings resembled each other, Austin was the only one who didn't have a tall, slight build. He was by no means overweight; he just had more bulk than his brothers. I believe that physical difference bothered him, and it affected his confidence.

Early in Austin's high school years, his family moved to Houston. We missed his warm presence in our student family. But then a few years later, Austin moved back to live with his grandparents during his senior year. He showed up at our big mudfest event right before school started. He was at least four to five inches taller, and he was toned and muscular from a year of running. I probably stood next to him for five minutes without recognizing him. Finally, he harassed me about not realizing who he was, and we spent a few minutes catching up on his life. He was still the same gregarious, thoughtful, capable person I'd known before, but now Austin saw that person, too. As with most adolescents, the physical changes that Austin experienced before he moved away had prompted questions of self-worth, purpose, and belonging that were answered only after he'd matured physically.

The process of individuation not only begins much earlier now, but it also takes longer to work through because the expected cultural age of adulthood has changed, too. Consider my father's story, for example. A few weeks after he graduated from high school, he packed his things, kissed his parents good-bye, and left the quiet little town of Bethany, Missouri. Six months later, he started working for Hallmark Cards in Kansas City. When he left Bethany, he had a strong sense of identity, he knew his choices mattered, and he understood how he could contribute to society. He had to get a job, find a place to live, pay his bills, build new friendships, do his own laundry, and deal with the annoyance of a hangover from the poker game the night before. At the age of 18, he was responsible for the whole of his life.

By the time my father graduated from high school in 1957, many of the issues of the who, what, and why of life were sufficiently answered, thus allowing him to transition smoothly from a teenager to an adult.

My, how things have changed! When students graduate from high school today, they still enter college, the military, or the workforce. But what's changed is that most 18-to-20-somethings are still financially connected to their parents. Living and education expenses aren't always costs that an 18-year-old can afford to pay alone—not to mention the fact that most entry-level jobs that are available to high school graduates today aren't typically positions that translate into lifelong careers. These circumstances often keep Mom and Dad involved in the young adult's monetary decisions. So one life arena that prevents a potential adult from seeking her own responsibility or success is finances.

Then there's the "home" dilemma. Living at home beyond the high school years and returning to sleep in her childhood bedroom during school breaks also complicates the dynamics of who's in charge. The most common complaint I hear from 19-year-olds is that their parents hassle them about staying out until dawn and then sleeping until noon the next day. The most common complaint I hear from parents about post-high schoolers is that they bring home a boatload of laundry, make a mess, and don't help with anything around the house.

Confused parents struggle between wanting the same amount of authority and influence in their kids' lives as when they were 16 years old, while also expecting them to demonstrate more adult responsibility. On the flip side, college students want the identity and privileges afforded to an adult, but they often revert back to the habits of their youth whenever they're home.

The succession of privileges and responsibilities in our culture seems strange to me. Pop culture encourages children to explore their sexuality via music lyrics, fashion trends, and movie themes by the time they're 13 or 14 years old. Sixteen-year-olds can drive, 18-year-olds can buy cigarettes and risk their lives for their country by serving in the military, but we all must wait until we're 21 to legally drink alcohol. And it's not until the ripe old age of 25 that "adolescent" insurance rates finally go down. What a strange progression of information and opportunity. No wonder they're confused!

This adolescent road trip is like being in the car with a little kid who asks, "Are we there yet?" every five minutes. I often wonder if that's how teenagers feel about their trek through adolescence. Am I there yet? Have I jumped through all of the necessary hoops to be considered worthy of the title of "adult"? Do I have what it takes to make it on my own? The balance between autonomy and authority gets a little tricky during these years. For adults, it's like a pendulum swinging wildly between the two realities, and it's difficult to know when to challenge teens to make more mature choices and when to encourage them to savor an unfinished childhood.

RATING THE PAIN

The ever-lengthening road to maturity takes its toll on adolescents' outlooks and emotions. They yearn for the freedoms of an adult, but they can't always adequately grapple with the responsibilities that accompany those freedoms. This leads to feelings of confusion and doubt about if and when choices and accountability will reconcile in their lives. Without a finish line in sight, teens feel anxious and uncertain. Thus, whenever they face obstacles, they quickly lose heart.

When children are injured or recovering from surgery, doctors sometimes show them a graph of facial symbols to help them rate the amount of pain they're feeling. It starts with a smiley face, which means there's no pain. And then the facial expressions gradually become sadder and sadder to represent an increase in pain. The last face appears to be very distraught, which means the pain is as bad as it can get. While this method may not provide a complete evaluation of pain, it's a good start.

If we were to "rate the pain" or struggle that adolescents face today, then we'd learn that the intensity of their trials and the level of their stress is far beyond what we experienced in the last couple of decades. They may have more perks and plusses in their lives—compliments of a society that continues to innovate and discover—but they also have more intersections where painful and difficult circumstances seem to stand in the way of a healthy journey.

From my perspective, the road to maturity is both an incredible and arduous path. It's a unique and remarkable season of life, as well as a road fraught with distractions and dangers. In *A Tribe Apart*, Patricia Hersch spends three years quietly walking alongside eight typical American high school students.[4] She tells their stories of living in a complex world of abundant opportunity and remarkable loss. Her powerful story of true adolescent experiences resonated with my own experience of walking alongside teens. It prompted me to consider this coexistence of good and bad news for my students. What do they gain in this brave new world they live in? What do they lose?

Abundant Opportunities

Accelerated, enhanced academics It's exciting for me to see students using more and more of their cerebral power. Whether by taking four Advanced Placement courses during their junior or senior years, or winning an international research scholarship at age 17, students are capable of excelling in an environment of challenge. It's a thrill to see average students take flight academically because someone raised the bar of excellence for them.

My daughter's second-grade class rarely required "seatwork." Most of the class time was spent on research, team projects, and answering how and why kinds of questions. Even math was integrated into complex problems that required critical thinking skills. More and more, education isn't just about conveying information, but teaching students how to think and discover information on their own. This is a growing strength in academics that will broaden the doors of opportunity for our students down the road.

Knowledge at their fingertips The community library may be the cultural anchor for gaining knowledge, but there's a virtual library of information available to students via television and the Internet. They can find information and entertainment on hundreds of cable channels, talk in real time to an Australian friend on Facebook, or find thousands of legitimate research sources for a senior thesis online. Knowledge access has a new face in our world, partially because of the ability to communicate and learn with the click of a mouse or the push of a cell phone button.

Sky's-the-limit technology In Louisville, Colorado, The DaVinci Institute has embarked on an incredible project called the Museum of Future Inventions.[5] When completed, this project will house pavilions that illustrate and explain the most important future developments in at least 12 different scientific fields. The goal of the museum is to literally transport visitors into the world of tomorrow, describing what life will be like once these inventions are realized. Some of the ideas they're envisioning include robots that recharge our home energy systems, a world of wireless power, a space elevator, machines that record dreams, technology-assisted telepathy, genetic cures for cancer and Alzheimer's, and much more.

I'm amazed at how much technology has advanced just since the days when I sat typing a paper on a bulky PC in college. Students of the twenty-first century have grown up in a fast-paced evolution of technology that will continue to shape their lives in a powerful way.

> I believe adolescents hear an incomplete and dangerous message about sexuality from the media. And the message is that their exposed sexuality defines their maturity.

Spending power It seems that more and more kids have increased access to their own money and their parents' money in American society. According to a 2007 article by Christine Lagorio, "8- to 12-year-olds spend $30 billion of their own money each year and influence another $150 billion of their parents' spending."[6] This might be because their parents are benefiting from their pursuit of the American Dream. Their innovation and hard work led to a life more comfortable than the one they experienced growing up. It might also be the result of a family living beyond their means on a lifeline of credit. Regardless of the reasons, many students are not only enjoying their parents' real or perceived success, but they're also able to pursue their own dreams with more resources.

Longer, healthier lives People are living longer. Medical advances that have improved child mortality rates and defeated once fatal diseases, improvements to simple things such as water sanitation, and the cultural awareness of healthier lifestyle habits that can add days to our lives all play a part in today's adolescents living longer. Their lives might even be void of some of the catastrophic illnesses that affected previous generations. In theory, our students will have more time to improve their lives and the lives of those around them, as well as more opportunities to impact their world for the greater good.

Global life experience I remember receiving letters from a pen pal in France when I was in junior high. We wrote letters back and forth for a while, describing our lives and exchanging pictures of our families and homes. And that was the extent of my global outlook as a child. Sure, I was learning about other places, memorizing my French vocabulary, and catching a sound bite here and there in the news about world affairs. But that was pretty much it. I didn't even leave the United States until I took my honeymoon cruise to the Bahamas (which is a beautiful destination, but not very far away!).

Now students experience and enter into cultures halfway around the globe through study abroad programs, mission trips, and family vacations. They can access a real-time view of distant places and people through Web cams, YouTube, Facebook, and MySpace. This new global life experience is helping a generation of young people think beyond themselves and about the impact their actions have on people living close and far away from them. It also encourages a desire to learn about and understand other cultures and combats tendencies toward prejudice.

Remarkable Loss

Fragmented families Families have changed in the last half-century. Some of the changes are positive, but many are difficult issues for youth to reconcile. One reality is that Mom and Dad aren't as involved in their kids' lives today as parents were several decades ago. Throughout society, parents are working longer and harder, sharing custody after a painful divorce, or serving a 12-month military deployment every few years. It's possible that some parents are trying to reclaim their own lost youth, struggling with drug or alcohol addictions, or just living a fast-paced, busy life apart from their children. Whether it's because of work, finances, divorce, preoccupations, misguided priorities, immaturity, poverty, or unavoidable circumstances, parents aren't taking or being given as many opportunities to participate in their kids' lives.

There have always been families who are pulled apart for one reason or another. But now the majority of students in our country experience divorce. Even though most adults acknowledge that the ending of a marriage is really difficult and stressful, the impact it has on students is often underestimated. A friend of mine endured a painful divorce about three years ago, and he did something that I find uncommon in my experience with dozens of divorced parents. Two years after the divorce, he and his girls were still going to counseling a few times a month. It was important to him that they all had ample time to walk—not run—through the big changes in their family's life, as well as wrestle with any confusion or pain those changes might bring. Rarely have I seen divorced families go for counseling longer than a few months. How can we expect a total of eight to twelve hours of counseling help us process a life-altering event?

The urgency parents feel to get past the messiness of divorce can show up in a new look, changed values and behaviors, and an abrupt entry back into the dating world. It makes sense to want to move on and put pain behind us—whatever that pain is. So we naturally, or unconsciously, assume that kids move on from a stressful or painful experience the same way adults do. But we absolutely must remember that a 13-year-old doesn't possess the same ability to understand, process, or adapt as an adult does. They'll suppress the events they can't emotionally accommodate. This can be a recipe for destructive behavior or emotional upheaval down the road—and usually when it's least expected. So it's important to remember that even though the issues causing family fragmentation are more commonplace now, we should never assume the individual effect on a child is any less distressing.

Competitive sports Recently, a local newspaper ran a story about summer workouts for several area high school athletic programs. In the article, a football coach recalled how one player's mom dragged him out of bed to go to an early morning practice because he'd overslept. The coach told the player that if he ever had to have his mom drag him to the mandatory practice again, he was off the team.

This coach's "football is your job" mentality and his demands that an adolescent make a very adult commitment to an extracurricular activity that will probably end when he finishes high school is troubling. For the student who never plays organized sports in college or beyond, the biggest impact of his high school athletic experience will be what it taught him about prioritizing, striving to excel, winning, losing, and working together with others.

Equally troubling is the mother who went so far as to force her son to go to practice and ultimately embarrassed him in front of the coach and quite possibly his teammates. Certainly part of adolescence is learning to finish well and follow through on commitments, but the natural consequences of sleeping through a morning workout would have been much healthier and more effective. This boy's lack of desire to be on the field promptly at 6 a.m. might be weariness, but it might also be a symptom of his mindset toward the sport he used to love.

Remember when neighborhood kids played pick-up games of baseball, basketball, or football? Remember when super sports heroes developed their love of the game at the park down the street, playing with friends, refereeing themselves, and coming back for more every day the weather allowed? I'm not sure those days exist anymore. I don't see them much in my neighborhood because just about every sporting activity that kids are in from first grade and beyond is organized and run by adults.

We schedule athletics into kids' lives with good intentions of teaching them a sport, beginning a lifestyle of personal fitness, and learning team camaraderie. But it doesn't take much for those good intentions to lose focus and perspective. When did it become okay for parents or coaches to yell at eight-year-olds during their first season of coach-pitch softball? Should we allow a cheerleading coach to curse at her squad during the state championships because they missed a crucial move in the routine?

Media-drenched sexuality I've noticed a current trend in the publicity and marketing of child stars. Some time during a female performer's mid to late-teen years, her music or acting suddenly exudes sensuality. It doesn't matter if her previous image was girly, athletic, comedic, or cutesy, because it seems the test for maturity in her art is to put her sexuality on display. There's no room for projects about her growing concern for orphaned children in a country torn apart by civil war, and there's very little encouragement to let her deepest passions about life become the most important thing people see.

Adolescence is a sensual experience. The desires and energy that teenagers feel as they become more in tune with their sexuality shouldn't be ignored. After all, they cannot remain children forever. However, adolescence is also an intellectual and a spiritual experience. Just as their sexuality is awakening, their minds are also better able to contemplate more deeply and their souls are hungry to connect with the things they cannot see. But somewhere in media land, someone sent down the memo to fixate adolescents on sexuality. One result has been a visual onslaught of sexual images and themes that lack truth and substance. Of most concern to youth workers is the fact that students get the message there's no such thing as healthy intimacy.

The reality is that sex sells. It sells in primetime on all of the major networks, where shows revel in sexual innuendo, if not explicit material. It sells on the Internet, where pornography addictions have reached epidemic proportions. Social networking sites are chock-full of seductive profile pictures and racy personal descriptions. It's the same with music. Songs and videos get more airtime when they push the boundaries of language and content.

I call it the distortion of the sacred. We're created to be drawn to sexuality. There's no shame in recognizing how we're wired or what we desire. But we seem to be easily lured into the distorted version of something that's meant to be so much more meaningful. I believe adolescents hear an incomplete and dangerous message about sexuality from the media. And the message is that their exposed sexuality defines their maturity.

Permeance of poverty There may be students who are enjoying the fruit of their family's financial success in today's culture, but there are also a growing number who are wondering if their lives have any options at all. The most important lesson I learned in working to help impoverished people is that it's really hard to escape poverty. Whereas a person with adequate resources often has family, savings, or other work opportunities to fall back on if she should suddenly lose her job, a person struggling to climb the steps out of poverty often lives with the reality that if her job doesn't work out, there's no safety net.

As someone who hasn't had to worry about where to find a good job or affordable insurance to protect my family, I absolutely must remember that there are people everywhere in my life who are just barely hanging on financially. As a youth worker, it doesn't matter to me whose fault it is because my priority is the children of the people who are facing financial difficulty—and it's never the children's fault.

Personal safety Life can and will be dangerous at times. There are personal tragedies, natural disasters, and wars in every generation. But for this generation, safety seems to be a daily stressor that puts dents in their lives. More than ever, students are concerned for their personal safety in groups, at school, and in their world. Bullies have always existed. But when we figure in larger schools where kids cannot be known as well by their teachers and administrators, suddenly the environment for bullying has a place to thrive. These bullying students are hurting, and they have no outlet to deal with their pain except to inflict it on someone else.

The threat of school violence lingers in their worries, too. I know it's a very different world today when my daughter's entire school district organizes annual drills to prepare for campus acts of violence. Adolescents must face the reality of terrorism not being some faraway problem for someone else to deal with, but a reality that can touch the doorsteps of their lives.

It's not just physical safety, either. It's also emotional safety. Oftentimes, teenagers don't feel safe sharing different ideas or living according to different values from their peers. These feelings lead students to compromise truth and integrity in exchange for acceptance. It's easier to fake an identity that doesn't draw attention or scrutiny. In dating situations, physical and emotional safety issues collide when a student becomes the victim of sexual violence. Such an experience can haunt a victim to the point that she'll evade a path to healing in order to avoid facing the reality of being attacked. Many of our students will face a life filled with physical and emotional danger.

Over- and under-the-counter drugs I remember when a student shared with me that his current drug of choice was inhaling fumes from toxic cleaners and paints. The weight of this circumstance left me feeling helpless when I realized he'd moved from more costly drugs like marijuana, which he purchased from a dealer in secret, to cheaper substances that are available at most local stores. I feared for his safety to the point of sleeplessness because I knew such highs could result in a quick and sudden death.

My parents live in a typical middle-class neighborhood in a metro area suburb. In the past five years on their street, a meth lab explosion in a neighbor's garage killed one of the residents, and agents from the Bureau of Alcohol, Tobacco, Firearms and Explosives (ATF) arrested a 19-year-old for running a large drug ring. Some of the most rampant use of homemade drugs is taking place in suburban and rural areas across the Midwest.

Students with substance abuse issues are searching for something. They could try drugs or alcohol recreationally and walk away without any damage. Unfortunately, if they can't stop using, the addiction will roar through their life like a runaway train.

EXIT RAMP

As people who lead students, we're searching for a way to anticipate and respond to this longer, harder season of maturity. How do we lead teenagers down a road of purpose, while entering into their real lives today? How do youth workers address the questions of a 12-year-old girl and a 17-year-old boy adequately and simultaneously? What can parents do to begin or rejuvenate their spiritual influence in their teenagers' lives? How can youth workers encourage and partner in that effort?

1. What aspects of today's adolescent journey are news to you? What differences do you see from your own adolescence?

2. When looking at the adolescents you know, do you see more remarkable opportunity or more abundant loss?

3. What do you believe parents wish youth workers understood about their journeys with their children? What do youth workers want to help parents understand about adolescent culture?

Embracing the Adolescent Road Trip

We loved you so much that we were delighted to share with you not only the gospel of God but our lives as well, because you had become so dear to us.
1 Thessalonians 2:8 (NIV)

CHAPTER

2

During my early years in youth ministry, sometimes I got so busy building the ministry or creating "groundbreaking" programs (chuckle, chuckle) that I lost sight of my real job description. I'm not referring to the list of duties given to me by the church. I'm talking about fulfilling Paul's legacy of loving people so much that he shared not only the message of Christ's love, but also their daily lives. His ministry took him into people's homes, where he sometimes stayed for weeks. That kind of proximity just begs for opportunities to really know people and experience regular intimate exchanges.

We've already concluded that adolescence is a remarkable but incredibly challenging journey. And most youth workers and parents would probably agree that delight is not the first word that comes to mind when contemplating our role in leading tweens and teens on their adolescent pilgrimage. Instead, we sometimes cope with teenage dilemmas by expressing sarcasm, retreating from leadership, or just functioning in a perpetual state of anxiety.

But Paul's words and example challenge us that it's both possible and necessary to find the delight in leading adolescents. Consider how the people Paul led were very much spiritual adolescents. They were young in their faith, they were quite confused about how to follow Christ and live in a pluralistic world, and they were constantly struggling in their relationships with one another. Yet he considered it a joy to live among them and point them to Christ and a life of deepest purpose.

WHAT'S IN A WORD?
Several things jump out at me from Paul's personal ministry description. First, it's not "he" that loved them so much but "we." Paul was being faithful to God's call on his life, but he wasn't doing it alone. He knew he couldn't possibly take care of everyone by himself, nor did he have all of the necessary abilities to lead this young church. A youth ministry partnership in our churches should extend from the youth worker to the parents and other caring adults who are willing to step onto the same road that the youth are walking.

Second, the verb *share* draws a beautiful picture of ministry. To share is to be communal and give mutually. That makes the idea of just telling someone about God's love and grace seem incomplete without a continued investment in dialogue and relationship. The message of the cross is powerful enough to draw people to belief—even if they hear it only once. But in his letters and repeated visits to early churches, Paul modeled ministry that didn't just help people step onto the road of faith, but also showed them how to walk it. For youth workers, the challenge might be to program less and relate more to youth and their parents. For parents, the challenge could be to figure out how to keep sharing life with their children even as they gradually let go of their need for parental input and direction.

Lastly, this life of ministry is no halfhearted endeavor. It requires that all of my life be available to the people I lead. I'm not referring to all of my time, but rather all of my heart and devotion. I have to let students see the real me while I'm living alongside them in the real world. There are days I feel silly because I miss the students and families I used to lead. But most days, I realize that to feel a vacancy in my heart today is to realize that I allowed these people to move in and reside in the rooms of my life for a time. So if I dare to follow Paul's example, my job is to share God's good news and my life with students and their families—and to include others in that task, too.

Somewhere along my journey of working with students, I decided I needed to embrace the fact that adolescence is a long road, get back to my sacred job description, and give parents and adults a deeper understanding of teenagers' travels toward maturity. This focus became an important first step to helping my students imagine for themselves a life of faith and purpose.

ROAD SIGNS FOR YOUTH WORKERS
Youth ministry is not a stage for youth workers. I'm a performer. As a sixth grader at First Baptist Church in Casper, Wyoming, I played the church organ and sang "We Are the Reason" for the Sunday night offertory. That was my very first performance. We tend to shy away from the word *performance* when referring to church music, but that's what it is—a performance for God, our audience of One. However, it easily gets misdirected as a performance in front of the congregation, which I'm sure is what happened to me on that summer evening. I forgot to turn on the microphone before I started playing, so the music minister had me do it again—with the microphone turned on this time—and that was it! I felt the thrill of creating music for people and receiving their accolades afterward. I was hooked!

After that first solo in grade school, I performed just about every day of my life until I began youth ministry. From talent shows and solo competitions in middle school and high school to hours of singing on a stage or in a rehearsal room in college, I was always "on" as a performer. Even when I was just walking past a mirror, I usually couldn't resist singing a few notes and critiquing what others heard and saw when I sang.

After college I soon sensed that God was pushing me backstage. I fought it at first, but whenever I tried to push my performance agenda in a ministry setting, it usually ended in either embarrassment or disaster for me. One time I packed my keyboard for a high school retreat, thinking I'd also be the cool worship leader. Never mind that I had plenty of other retreat details to manage and not enough time to prepare. Well, it was really bad. I'm a good singer, but I don't play the piano well in front of others—especially unrehearsed! When we finished what was probably a painful worship set for the students, an honest 16-year-old looked at me and said, "Denise, don't quit your day job!"

God was patiently redirecting my focus to an audience of One. I still had outlets for my music, but I began to understand two things: The students needed me to be alongside them in their lives, not in front of them. Sure, I still needed to teach lessons and give messages. But none of the students seemed to remember what marvelous things I taught them; they just remembered that I was there.

Lots of us love to be in front of the crowd, and there are healthy and effective avenues for that gift. But we're not all working in Nashville to record a hit song or traveling the country speaking to thousands of people. Youth ministry cannot be our personal outlet for impressing, performing, or upstaging others. It must be a platform for launching God's love and hope into students' lives.

Youth ministry is not about a formula that equals results. I had a love-hate relationship with an annual ministry report that I was required to complete. The form contained a list of weekly ministry programs and school grades with a blank next to each item. And the instructions asked us to quantify how many students we had enrolled in each program. The request for these yearly statistics wasn't a horrible church crime, but rather a tool for measuring growth in our denomination. Just the same, I cringed at filling out this report every year because I couldn't quantify so many things on paper. Do I include the eleventh grader who comes to worship service with his mom only a few times a month? He wasn't really an active participant, but he'd been going out for coffee with our high school intern once a month. Or should I leave off the kids who'd been baptized and became members after confirmation but who then—along with their families—dropped off the radar more than a year ago?

I know it's important to have a plan and a vision for our ministries and then measure our effectiveness accordingly. But I found myself relying on the structure of the formula and the answers to quantifiable questions more than I trusted in the sometimes invisible imprint we leave on students' lives. I'd find a strong ministry formula and develop it with our students and leaders, and then I'd wait for remarkable, visible results.

Quite often there were visible results, which only motivated us to focus all of our ministry energy on tangible outcomes. If no students raised their hands to commit their lives to Christ at the fall retreat, then we leaders believed we didn't effectively deliver the message of the gospel that weekend. But in reality, a 15-year-old student was there and heard the gospel for the first time. He didn't feel safe enough to raise his hand in front of a group of strangers, but the message still moved him. He went home, sat down on his bed, and simply prayed for God to show him how to follow Christ. The faith journey that began that night in his room wouldn't become a church conversion statistic until he responded to an invitation to baptism during his sophomore year in college—at a different church.

When I realized that God can keep track of who's searching for him and who's responding to him, I discovered a deeper well of hope within me for every student I encountered. I also recognized the absurdity of believing my formula for ministry would make or break God's kingdom.

Youth ministry is not the same as parenting. Those of us who work with students as professionals or volunteers tend to unconsciously act as though parents should just follow our lead in relating to their teenagers. We meet parents once, give them the "I understand your child better than you do" handshake, and then in a helpful—but sometimes patronizing—fashion we imagine we're taking over pointing the way. I was much more prone to do this before I had kids of my own. And I'd get irritated with parents who told me, "You'll understand when you have your own kids."

The funny thing is, they were right! I really love teenagers as a group, and sometimes I've had a deep affection for individual students over the years. But none of those relationships come close to how I felt the day my daughter was born. I struggled to put into words the extraordinary connection I felt with Lanie Grace the first time I held her. I wept for a lack of any other means of expressing the burst of emotion that engulfed my soul. And that connection is why I freak out when I'm worried for her safety; it's the cause of my empathizing tears when she realizes a schoolmate no longer wants to be her friend; and it sometimes blinds my long-term perspective. I realize that I'm now that parent who is crazy or who has tunnel vision or who just needs to calm down.

Although there is plenty of room and need in teenagers' lives for youth workers and adult mentors, deep down they're still hoping for some guidance and help from Mom and Dad. Obviously, things can go very wrong in a family and cause our students to look for others to walk alongside them. But I've never met a student who wished for a bad or nonexistent relationship with a parent. He or she may have wished it was different or better, but that fact should motivate us to build bridges in families and let parents be the heroes whenever possible.

Youth ministry is a relay. During any given Sunday morning of my last few years of ministry at Redeemer Covenant Church, the high school students experienced Bob Ogle's passionate and detailed teaching of Scripture, Joyce McCormick's lively spiritual and philosophical class discussions about God's kingdom and character, Martha King's funny and insightful lessons about how knowing Christ should transform our way of living, or Mike King's rare ability to present all of his seminary knowledge in a way that students can understand. Then they were invited into moments of prayer and worship as Evan Gundy led a group of student musicians. And the morning wrapped up with a few more minutes of sharing and discussion with other adult leaders. Usually, all I did was offer a quick welcome, share any announcements, and then fill in when a leader couldn't be there.

> But Paul's words and example challenge us that it's both possible and necessary to find the delight in leading adolescents.

During the week, students could participate in a house group, where they typically shared life with people like Rick and Susan Grapengater, Debi Caldwell, Summer Pecaut, Carolyn Hellstern, Ranae and Stan Bugh, Joe Hart, the Rutherfords, and Nancy Mankin. And if students participated in leadership stuff, then they got to experience Evan Gundy and Lana Roskamp, who teamed up with me to lead on Wednesday nights.

So often, we treat youth ministry as a which we're running against each other to see whose ministry will win. But really, it's more like a relay—we carry the baton of teaching or leading for a while, and then we pass it on to another equally capable teammate. I found that when I really applied the "we" part of Paul's statement, "we loved you so much," our ministry was able to coach adolescents in their spiritual training and surround them with true Christian examples and a loving community that encouraged them to keep going.

In writing this book, I sent out some questions to student alumni about growing up at Redeemer. One of my former students, Ryan Myers, has a unique perspective because he now has my old job as Director of Student Ministry at Redeemer! His response to the question about who made a big difference in his life and faith is a great testimony to encouraging lots of adults to pour into students' lives:

> As far as people who really impacted and encouraged me and my faith, I would say you, Gary, Eric Mills, Bill Clark, Bob Ogle, Mike Cunningham, and Joyce McCormick did a lot for me during that time of quick growth and questioning. In addition to these folks, the Secrests, Wakefields, Gotchers, and Goulds were huge forces in my life during that time as well.

I count the names of at least 15 adults who helped shape Ryan during his teenage years. And now Ryan is doing for his students what he remembers so many others doing for him!

Youth ministry should help students find their place in God's Story. I didn't grow up in a church tradition of confirmation. But when I came on staff at Redeemer, it was a strong emphasis in the middle school ministry. So I had to work through my own questions and concerns about the purpose and impact of a confirmation class. While I still have concerns that confirmation sometimes becomes one of those formulas we rely on more than the movement of God in kids' hearts, I found I could embrace Redeemer's approach to confirmation because it certainly seemed to fulfill exactly what it means "to be sure."

The entire purpose of this yearlong study was to share God's Story with students so they could have the opportunity to enter into that Story and be sure of what they believed about the message of salvation. At the end, students stood before the congregation and were affirmed in their completion of the class and given a new study Bible to help them continue growing and learning about God. We confirmed their personal decisions to embrace the gospel during individual interviews the week before, so students who weren't yet ready to make a decision to follow Christ could abstain with integrity and without embarrassment. We also reminded the students that we cared about the whole of their lives and would continue to encourage them in their faith.

I appreciate ministry environments where we meet our students wherever they are and with no requirements for their participation, attendance, or membership attached to the gospel message.

ROAD SIGNS FOR PARENTS

For parents, it can be easy to allow the difficult days of guiding an adolescent to overshadow the beautiful and momentous parts of the journey. Youth workers can play a vital role in encouraging moms and dads to rediscover their eternal influence with their teenagers during the years when many parents seem to relinquish it. These "signs" are thoughts I humbly share as truths I hold on to in my own parenting and share with other parents on the same path. It's all about remembering to delight in our children's growing-up journey, even when it's a not-so-delightful path for the parents or the children.

The adolescent road is not a dreaded survival expedition! Okay, now it's true that parents can be completely in survival mode some days: Communication with their teenager is terrible, the choices the teenager makes are poor, and, quite frankly, Mom and Dad feel like they're going to go right over the edge!

The key is not to anticipate the adolescent years in a negative way. We've all done it. We describe the teen years the same way we described the terrible twos. "Teenager" becomes a code word among adults for, "Oh, she's at that age! Good luck, and I hope you survive!" That kind of banter cuts to the heart of a teen's confidence. It communicates that we don't really want to walk this road alongside her. And that could be her cue to find another influencer who will show more interest.

The adolescent experience is not a resume-building endeavor. This is a tough one to steer clear of because a whole lot of well-meaning parents want to help their teenagers make the most out of these formidable developmental years in academics, sports, activities, and even job experiences. It's natural to want to help teens prepare for success in college and their future careers. But the truth is that who they become is so much more important than what colleges they get into or how much money they could earn.

I love to ask students, "Who will you be in 10 years?" instead of asking them what they want to do when they grow up. I'm not suggesting that parents abandon encouraging their children to participate in activities and pursuits that can lead to their future success. They just shouldn't allow it to become an obsession or the sum total of who their children are as 16-year-olds.

The adolescent road is not one that parents can travel for their kids. Dad can't be his son's alternate in this race. He can't learn the difficult lessons for his son. Or consider it this way—as a wise friend once shared with me—"You can't choose the mistakes he will make." Although as parents we can be supportive and offer our children advice, there are some dilemmas we won't be able to fix. Of course, there might be circumstances in which we absolutely must run interference and be advocates for our teenagers. There are definitely times when intervention is necessary because a teen's health and safety are at risk. There are internal alarms and gut checks for those circumstances. But most of the time, it's important to help parents remember that repeated rescues encourage an unhealthy reliance, while leading by letting go encourages learning and independence.

The adolescent experience is a time-release journey. "Time-release" capsules release their medicine into the body a little at a time until the entire capsule or dose has been used. In much the same way, adolescence is a long process in which a teenager slowly embraces more accountability and receives more privileges as a result. Throughout this process parents need encouragement to let go, little by little—even when we may believe we have a better plan.

Our sons and daughters need room to breathe as individuals, to make difficult decisions that will leave an imprint on their souls, and to learn lessons that will shape the people they're becoming. This is not to say Dad and Mom should relinquish all influence when their children turn 15! Adolescence is a long bridge to adulthood, and teens need their parents to go all the way across with them—sometimes following at a healthy distance.

The adolescent road is a path every one must travel. It's not just what a neighbor's kid is going through—all must travel this road, and it's difficult and wonderful for everyone along the way. There are weeks—and sometimes even a month here or there—when everything is blissful. Then there are excruciating days that seem never-ending. A student's access to affluence, information, or experience rarely eases the difficulty of the adolescent journey. Nor does an especially sheltered life make the journey risk-free. He may be an articulate, accomplished student and still feel an overwhelming pressure to perform. She could be a standout athlete with accolades and opportunity, but an unspoken pain may lurk in the shadows of her heart. Every adolescent in our culture is traveling on this road toward adulthood, and it helps them so much when their parents gain perspective and show empathy for the many challenges of this journey.

ROAD SIGNS FOR US ALL

On the lonely road through adolescence, there's nothing better than when young travelers continually encounter more and more adults who are willing, ready, and delighted to step onto the road and walk beside them for a while. As people who lead adolescents, let's gently help one another watch for these "road signs" and take them to heart in the hope of seeing the adolescents we care about be transformed.

Adolescence is a life-shaping pilgrimage. This is why I love the adolescent age! So many things come together during these years. Students have an amazing capacity to mature in their understanding of themselves, their beliefs, and their world when they embark on this journey. This extended season of growing up may not have existed several hundred years ago, but biology and culture have ushered it in. This presents a remarkable opportunity to help young people navigate these experiences that will resonate throughout their lifetimes. When we see it through that lens, we can more fully enjoy the days of plenty and endure those days when we find the students we know wandering in the barren wilderness.

Adolescence is a road where all the lanes eventually merge. All the academic hurdles, social obstacles, bumpy emotional terrain, and spiritual questioning are connected. The loss of a friendship can lead her to faith questions about loneliness and abandonment. A persistent challenge in school can cause him to question his worth and ability to succeed. A broken relationship with a parent can impede her schoolwork or cause detours in her intimate relationships. All these things affect each other and can work in cooperation to help or hinder growth. When looking at one area of a student's life, we must recognize all the life lanes that may be intersecting in that specific situation.

EXIT RAMP

On a recent anniversary trip, my husband and I hiked in Devil's Den State Park in the Ozark Mountains. For part of the day, we joined a guided tour of the crevices and caves that are scattered all over the park. It was exhilarating to climb and crawl through the openings and hear how they were created from shifting plates of the ancient mountains. On the way home, we decided we should return and take our daughter, Lanie, through those crevices and caves, now that we knew the trail to follow. We knew that if we had problems or questions when we returned, that same guide would be there to assist and even go along with us if we needed him to.

When I try to describe the role of mentoring adults and parents in students' lives, this story seems like a good example. The hope is that youth workers can partner with moms and dads to point the way for their adolescent children on an unfamiliar road and across rough terrain. But leading their kids through adolescence is often new territory for parents. That's where guides such as teachers, youth workers, coaches, and mentors play a vital role.

It's a good thing for parents and students to lean on the knowledge and friendship of a guide who knows and understands the adolescent landscape. It's also a very good thing for guides to help navigate the road and go along for the ride with students and parents—or even lead for however long they're needed. And when this ideal scenario isn't possible for a student, we want to make sure to find an adult leader who's able to step on the road and walk the distance with that teenager.

As your mile marker guide, I'd like to welcome you to the adolescent road trip!

1. What's one word or phrase that describes your strongest emotion about helping children travel to maturity via the road of adolescence?

2. Which road signs do you identify with the most?

3. Which road signs do you believe are more common?

4. How can youth workers and parents help each other lead the kids they love?

Marking Their Miles

"Set up road signs; put up guideposts.
Mark well the path by which
you came."
Jeremiah 31:21a (NLT)

CHAPTER

3

MILE MARKERS ON THE ADOLESCENT ROAD TRIP

When I'm traveling down a highway, I always notice the mile markers. Maybe it's because they were so prevalent on the landscape of my childhood home in Wyoming. I distinctly remember the audible whoosh I heard each time our car sped past those small green signs. When I was a little girl it seemed like our family could drive the 180 miles on Interstate 25 between Casper and Cheyenne without seeing more than a handful of cars in either direction. When I thought we might never get there, another numbered stake in the ground would zoom by my backseat window. Against a backdrop of blowing sagebrush, scattered mountains, roadside oil wells, and an occasional antelope sighting, the consistent and progressive rhythm of mile markers on the landscape assured me that we were getting closer to our destination.

I believe the adolescent journey is a lot like a road trip through the Wyoming wilderness. It's definitely an adventure, but it's also a long way for students to travel from the angst of early adolescence to an age of confidence in who they are and what they believe. All students want to get to the promised land of adulthood, but they have to do some wandering before they get there. The longer the pilgrimage, the more opportunities will arise for them to lose their way or follow a dangerous detour. But a longer journey also allows for more celebration of miles traveled, which can in turn spur them on toward the goal.

Adolescence is a sometimes sacred, sometimes mundane, sometimes exuberant, and sometimes dark journey; and the movement between these contrasting personal realities can be quick and unexpected. One day a student might feel beautiful and strong; but on the very next day, a cruel word is all it takes for her to see herself as ugly and weak. A moment of triumph can quickly give way to utter defeat, as a student's confidence and forward-looking attitude can revert to second-guessing himself after a quick change in the scenery around him.

Help Them Hear the Whoosh

So how do we help teenagers not only discover, but also anchor their purpose and identity on the path to maturity? As youth workers who lead and influence for only a short time, how do we help the good and the bad parts of this journey resonate throughout our students' lives in a meaningful way? How do we help them cross paths with many adults who can speak into their lives? What can we do to help parents come alongside their kids as life coaches and spiritual guides?

Just as those numbered green signs reassured my restless spirit on a wilderness road trip, students need adults in their lives who can help them hear the whoosh of signs that mark pivotal moments on their journey through the adolescent wilderness. They need their own mile markers to keep pressing on—road signs and guideposts not made of materials but of life experiences that remind them of where they've come from, who they are right now, and why their destination is worth the trip. As they continue farther down the road, they need to hear the whoosh again and again. Mile markers is the practice of leading students toward personal, tangible, and memorable moments that help shape the person they're becoming. When we point them to these big and small experiences, we help them discover answers to those questions of identity, purpose, and community, which then advance them down the road of maturity.

When I think of the significant mile markers I had the opportunity to offer to my students, I think about sitting across the table from a seventh grader named Jaymee as she fired off her theological inquiries and took notes on everything I said and all that we discussed and discovered together. I think about coming alongside Francie and Lauren as they ventured into the unknown territory of organizing their friends to prepare, deliver, and serve a meal to the local homeless shelter. I remember listening to Jason's story of choosing to follow Christ and the way he challenged his peers to do the same following his 2 a.m. testimony at one of our middle school all-nighters. I reminisce about the smiles on my students' faces just because I showed up at their homecoming pep rally to celebrate the day and meet their friends.

Roadbed Construction

My husband's parents live in Inola, Oklahoma. It's a small town about 15 miles east of Tulsa. When I think of Inola, I picture the sign that boasts HAY CAPITAL OF THE WORLD! and a railroad track that runs the entire length of the town. My kids are delighted to go there and hear the *choo choo* of trains all day and night.

In order for the railroad tracks to hold up under the burden of the many trains that chug through town each day, the foundation underneath—the roadbed—must be strong and stable. That roadbed in Inola has been the foundation for locomotion traffic for almost 120 years now.

There are lots of good youth ministry "tracks" out there that point students to a life of following God. Much like a roadbed, mile markers offer a foundation that's meant to strengthen whatever good ministry track is already being followed. It's an intentional and frequent practice of coming alongside an individual student or a group of adolescents and asking yourself questions such as, *Where are students on their journey toward adulthood? How can I help them drive another stake in the ground that anchors their faith, purpose, and identity?* Using mile markers is an exercise in living with these kinds of questions and discovering how the answers are best demonstrated in the lives of the students we care about.

All youth workers would probably like to say that they began their youth ministries intentionally asking these kinds of questions, but the questions often find us instead. For me, it was during a mission trip to Mexico when the local missionary leaders seemed frustrated with my team's attitude. I knew that some of the students came on the trip just to get out of town, and others weren't being respectful toward the local leaders. The challenges didn't discourage me. These students didn't all fit the "church kid" temperament that the missionary leaders were used to, so I searched for ways to help the adults better understand these students whom I really cared about.

First, I intentionally demonstrated my genuine care for the students by celebrating their interests and strengths. I made sure the local leaders heard me point out the individual strengths of each teenager and utilize any skills that were appropriate for the trip.

Second, I had a private conversation with the local leaders asking for their patience and willingness to see God at work in these kids' lives, even though they were an unusual group for the missionary leaders to host.

That Mexico mission trip was just the beginning of understanding my students' unique adolescent experiences. At home, I continued to clarify their stories. Like many American kids, my students had much to be thankful for: Successful and generous parents, beautiful homes, nice cars, educational advantages, extracurricular opportunities, and world travel, to name just a few. For some, there were also obstacles that caused them to stumble: Busy family lives, recreational drug use, self-injury, neglected relationships, and casual sexual choices. This dual existence of abundance and loss seemed to leave many teenagers with antagonizing doubts. The exterior veneer of their lives was an overlay of good things, but those good things alone couldn't define their interior purpose or significance. Therefore, many not-so-good things began to fill that internal void. Their church participation didn't always make the difference, either. They might have been present physically, but internally their lives were unraveling emotionally and spiritually.

My students needed help pushing aside all of their stuff so they could see a God who cared only about them, not their performance or affluence. They needed the opportunity to truly embrace the good news they heard every week in our ministry. They needed to walk in the shoes of people with fewer worldly possessions who could show them true spiritual wealth. They needed a chance to sacrifice for the sake of another. Along with their parents and siblings, they needed encouragement and help to rediscover what it means to be a family, even when things go wrong.

Those were some of the mile markers that I realized my students needed to experience together throughout our ministry. In addition, each of them needed different or more specific guideposts to help their journeys. For one of my students, this meant providing a safe place for him to ask questions, since he'd never heard about Jesus before. For another student, it was helping him figure out life after his mom died and quietly supporting him through a loss he chose to keep private. For yet another, it was recognizing that her world had just been transplanted to a new neighborhood, a new high school, a new group of friends, and a new church.

I have an unwritten list of some important mile marker opportunities that I missed in my early years of youth ministry. For one student, I missed a chance to offer him hope and accountability in his struggle with alcohol by sending a well-intentioned but overly stern letter. Instead, he should have seen a group of caring adults gather around him for support and intervention. For another, I missed the chance to demonstrate God's unfailing grace to her when she was acting erratically and intimidating her peers. I didn't recognize the deeper agonies she carried in her heart. And other times, I'd just do an event and not prayerfully consider if it was what any of my students needed.

Thankfully, I've had good moments to let God redeem some of those misses, and I'm still trying to work my way through that list and retrace my steps in those students' lives whenever I can.

Asking the Impossible

There are times when we feel particularly ill-equipped to meet all of the needs of the students in our care. We might have to go on emotional autopilot for a while when others are hurting and need us to be strong. But then, when we least expect it, we must face our own pain. We may even experience the good stress of a thriving ministry, but we still want to give up because we cannot possibly take care of everyone.

During one very tough year, our ministry lost a college student and a high school student in two separate fatal car accidents. Even months later, the pain still lingered and seemed to permeate every moment of my ministry. I walked into my senior pastor's office one day with a heavy heart. He met weekly with each staff ministry leader to encourage us and debrief current ministry issues. I told him that I wondered if I should go back to leading music and performing because it was so much easier for me to succeed in that area. My boss and friend gave me words that I still hold onto today: "Denise, God only calls you to the things that you cannot accomplish without him."

As obvious and simple as this truth seems, I found that I was often trying to reach a world of teenagers for God—without God's help or sustenance. There we were, deep in the adolescent wilderness, and I was overwhelmed by the ministry program and the needs of the students. Even during our joyful seasons of ministry, I felt as though the only way to reach all of the students and meet all of the needs was to streamline our curriculum and programs and ask volunteers to duplicate my style. But not everyone was at the same place in their adolescent journey; and not every volunteer leader was wired like me to enjoy or succeed in the managed chaos of my lessons, games, and events.

This is the struggle of youth ministry; we often lead more students than we can possibly know and shepherd. Even if there are only 15 to 20 students in our care, that's more than Jesus led personally—and he had a distinctly Divine advantage! The efficient role for us to play is the up-front leader, because from there we can be visible, organize, inspire, and point the way for many. That kind of leadership is definitely needed, but ministry must go beyond directing people and program traffic.

But this goal of personally knowing every student in our group and sharing the gospel and our lives with them is impossible for one person to accomplish. That's why the practice of mile markers invites the presence of many different guides to take the journey with students. Mile markers offer a path of incarnational ministry for parents, church elders, new moms, busy dads, college mentors, young couples, empty nesters, and more. It's a shepherding approach that's less about being in front of the group and more about walking with students to protect and guide them. When adults walk alongside students, we're best able to leave God's imprint on their lives because we know where they actually are on this journey.

One of my former students, Adam Butler, who is now in vocational ministry, wrote about all of the guides who shepherded him through adolescence:

> My time at Redeemer turned my whole life around. I experienced a group of people who didn't fit the mold of Christians I'd met since moving to Oklahoma. There, I experienced people who listened, as well as people who cared. Denise, Tim, John, Sandra, Bill and Debi Caldwell, and Joyce McCormick are the people who come to mind. I find myself still going back to Joyce's lessons for talks sometimes. My time working with junior high students under John, as well as just hanging out with him, was essential in my spiritual journey. I knew I could always count on Denise to be honest with me. Tim did an amazing job of listening to my story and asking great questions. Bill and Debi showed me what it meant to be a part of the church. Sandra Miller always asked me good questions and was always a friend.

Four of the seven people Adam listed were staff members who each—in different ways and at different times—led Adam down the road of becoming an adult. The other three were volunteer leaders who modeled faith in real life for countless students. If I'd been the only person who reached out to Adam, then you can imagine what treasures he would have missed.

Our job in youth ministry is not to know every student, but rather to make sure every student is known and cared for by a leader who can share life with him or her. That's when mile markers make an eternal impact, because the guiding person has seen a student's life at ground zero and knows what burdens she's carrying, what questions linger on her heart, and what dreams she's praying God will bring to fruition. Our leadership is most transformative when we pledge to lead many but minister to one student at a time. It's not the easiest ministry road to take, but I believe it's the most valuable.

ROAD SIGNS

Whatever new and bright ideas we implement, it's important to remember that students don't keep coming and bringing friends to our group just because they had a great time, heard an amazing message, or did something crazy. They may come once or twice for those reasons, but they keep coming back because they encounter something that makes a difference for them individually. They show up because they're yearning for another experience that will give them strength, help them understand, or point the way. In order to answer the question of how to lead students to personal, memorable, and tangible mile marker moments, someone has to pay attention to the students' lives and their surroundings.

Survey the Landscape

At the risk of sounding like a travel advertisement, Wyoming's expansiveness is not due to its sprawling number of square miles alone, but also to the vastness of its landscapes. In the northeastern part of the state, Devil's Tower intimidates the grasslands as an impossible natural rock creation. The Red Desert in the southwest boasts sand dunes with an ancient volcano rising from within called Boar's Tusk. In the gateway southeast, wheat fields and mountain ranges take turns dominating the horizon, while the Cathedral Group peaks in the Grand Teton mountain range keep watch over the springs and geysers of Yellowstone National Park in the northwest. All of these unique places are a part of Wyoming, but the scenery radically changes from one region to another.

In a similar way, even though our students are all in the wilderness of adolescence, their surrounding landscapes can be really diverse. Therefore, it's important that we survey the landscapes of their lives and observe what they're seeing and experiencing every day. What general adolescent issues are specific struggles for them? What unique and personal stories do those struggles fit into?

A snapshot of one particular class of students in my ministry could be described as a traveling party of personalities. They attended the same school, enjoyed each other's company, and showed up en masse to Sunday mornings and their house groups. It didn't matter what games we played or where we played them, this group's goal was to cheat and get caught. Their weekly challenge soon became seeing how creatively they could cheat and how big a reaction they could get. They were loud, funny, and, not surprisingly, guarded about the real issues they faced in their lives.

I really loved this class because they were fearless and outlandish, but I couldn't always draw them out effectively. So I stepped to the sidelines and let my friend and Young Life leader, Brian, invite them to journey with him. He was the listener when they needed some real conversations about their very real struggles, the teacher who challenged them to strive for more, and the very real incarnation of Christ in their lives.

Within this same class were students with strong leadership potential, others who showed up craving the serious stuff, and a handful who attended different high schools from everyone else. The student leaders needed their strength to be nurtured and put into action. The thinkers saw no point in the games we played, dove into the discussion questions with intimidating certainty, and needed an invitation to step out of the "spiritual giant" role and talk about their doubts, family situations, and private struggles. Those students who attended other schools needed a greater sense of community that could draw them into the weekly revelry. In order for us to have an effective ministry, it was vital that we leaders recognized the fact that this class had not only a charismatic overall group dynamic, but it was also made up of unique individual students who shouldn't be lumped in with the rest of the crowd. Our students needed to be seen as individuals—each one of them had a compelling story to tell.

Gauge Their Pace

I've run the Inola Run with my husband, Gary, several times now. It's an 8k event that loops out of town on farmland roads and back. I'm a decent runner, but I'm not built for speed or heat. I love to run when it's a brisk winter day, but I hate to run when the temperature nears the century mark because it can give me a terrible headache.

Regardless of my running preferences, Gary always talks me into running this race in his hometown. It usually falls on a hot June evening with no breeze on the shadeless course. The first year I ran it, I actually thought I might be lost on that rural Oklahoma road forever until the turnaround finally came into sight—and with a merciful water station beckoning my overheated body. When I looked at the stats after I crossed the finish line, I was surprised to see that I was fourth in my age category. Wow! Maybe I'm better at this than I thought. Maybe I'm improving my pace. A few seconds later, I realized there were only four runners in my age category.

Students aren't really sure how they're doing either. Nor are we adults always sure for them. When observing them alone or together, it's important to know what their pace is on the adolescent journey. Not all adolescents are ready for the same challenges, lessons, leadership, discipline, or even mentoring.

Let me offer a few examples. In leading a discussion with middle school students about guys and girls, a sixth grade boy blurted out, "I don't know why we're talking about this. I don't even like girls!" Yet in that same group of students, there were several eighth grade girls who I worried were (based on the stories I'd heard) already making some risky choices with guys.

Another year, numerous girls from the senior class attended a house group where they were working through studies that required daily reading and devotions. Most were ready for this kind of a challenge, in part because of the adult mentors who'd influenced their lives thus far. But a few girls felt out of place in that environment. They had an awkward history with the group leaders, and they needed a different approach to small groups than our discussion and prayer format. They'd had endured some real sorrows in their short lives, and too few people had taken the time to enter into their brokenness. I still wish I'd stepped onto their road and walked with them much earlier than I did. When I did invite these girls to meet me for coffee every Monday at 9 P.M., they immediately accepted the invitation. We didn't do a specific study that year. We didn't always venture into spiritual topics. I just bought them food and sat across the table from them each week, listening to them talk to each other and sometimes to me. But I know God met them in those conversations; I know they'll always remember that someone walked alongside them with no pressure, no guilt, and no strings attached.

Go Before, Go With, or Stay Behind
Our student leadership program, called "Leadership Project," was a bit unconventional for several reasons. First, students weren't voted for or chosen. Anyone could apply for it, as long as their applications were turned in by the midnight deadline. And I never excluded anyone. I only asked that they examine their own hearts and lives and then remove themselves from the team if they couldn't fulfill the obligations of time, teamwork, and example. I figured there were plenty of other places where students are told they can't be a part of something or aren't good enough to do something, so Leadership Project (LP) would be a place where, if they were willing to rise to the challenge, God could use any of them!

Secondly, LP success was dependent on student commitment and follow-through, not adults picking up the slack. The whole purpose of calling it the Leadership Project was to make it a learning path of trial and error. I tried not to do the work that they were capable of doing. Adult leaders had to resist making decisions that the students were ready to make, even if we would've done it differently. However, students did have to stay within a budget and demonstrate how their ideas fit in with our student ministry purpose and values.

We had some endeavors that fell flat, but we also had some wonderful successes. I'm most proud of Cinco de Bando (their twist on the Spanish!), a now-annual outdoor music event that showcases five local high school or college bands that play for free. There's a $5 admission charge that goes completely toward a mercy mission organization somewhere in the world. They design their own T-shirts to sell, ask the bands to play, do all the advertisements, find an emcee, set up, tear down, and clean up the trash in the dark after everything is done.

In guiding students toward mile markers, it's important that we adults not only check out the teenagers' surroundings and notice their stride on the adolescent road, but also determine the place where we should lead them. Do we go out to the front and beckon them to follow us? Do we walk in step with them and decide where to go next together? Or do we fall back at a safe and accessible distance and let them navigate for a while? It all depends on other variables in their journey, but it's yet another step in helping them build confidence in themselves and take ownership of their destination.

WELL-WORN PATHS

My friend Lana has a gift for drawing beautiful word pictures. She and I often talk about our hopes and dreams for students. One of her hopes is to give students "well-worn paths" that they can easily come back to if they take a detour or get stranded on their journey toward adulthood.

When I was in elementary school in Casper, Wyoming, I remember taking a class field trip to a portion of the Oregon Trail that meanders across the state from east to west. In some places along the trail, there are deep, unmistakable ruts in the ground where the wagons and horses and people followed the path of those who'd gone West before them. If they somehow veered off the trail, then it would be easy to know when they encountered it again. Mile marker experiences can guide our students in a similar way.

Here are some "paths" that might serve as significant mile markers as we help students on their journey.

Memories That Anchor Them

Students love to reminisce and relive special moments. They have an uncanny ability to keep celebrating a past event while still living in the present and striving for the future. Once we get older, we tend to try to make the present and future look more like the past. So give students memories. Make sure they remember laughing, crying, accomplishing, trying, changing, going, giving, and learning. These memories will anchor their perspective and lift the fog of indifference and indecision.

I remember the day I was supposed to hang out with Kristin Kindred. She was a fairly new driver, and I bravely told her I wanted a ride to lunch. Sadly, the day of our scheduled meeting turned out to be the day I gave the eulogy at her funeral after a tragic car accident. Instead of talking with Kristin about her hopes and dreams for the future, I spent the morning at Panera Bread Company with about eight of her close friends, listening to their stories. They introduced me to the cinnamon crunch bagel, and we shared our grief and joy together. On that summer morning, through our tears and laughter, our lives were knit together in an enduring memory that we've often returned to as we celebrate Kristin's life and how God carried us in that loss.

> Our job in youth ministry is not to know every student, but rather to make sure every student is known and cared for by a leader who can share life with him or her.

Ah-Ha! Moments

Students need not only memories, but also moments where that light in their brains flips on. Give a student room to discover a new idea or truth that becomes part of who he is. The impact of him discovering a truth on his own is much more powerful than just telling him about it. One way to do that is to remove comfort and familiarity in expectations and surroundings.

I'm always thrilled at how an urban mission trip challenges student and adult attitudes about poverty and the part they can play in the solution. Students usually leave their hometown having rarely ever ventured to a poorer part of town because they've always heard it's "dangerous over there." Then they spend several days and nights in a new city, living fully immersed in the culture they'd been taught to avoid. They usually return home empowered to genuinely care for homeless people and willing to sacrifice more for the sake of a struggling stranger.

So What? Exits

When my staff taught students, our goal was twofold: Impart truth into their lives and leave them wondering. We wanted some question or thought to bug them all week. We wanted them to search for the reasons the lesson was important to their lives. A personal search for the "So what?" leaves a much greater imprint on their souls than any words or activities can.

Several times during my youth ministry life, a female student would call me or email me with a question about women in ministry. Usually, she was asking because someone questioned the validity of her having a female youth minister. Now, that's a topic I could easily share my strong convictions about and tell her exactly why the other person was wrong. However, even on the biblical issues that invite much debate and discussion, I still want my students to read and study for themselves and trust God to give them understanding. So each time this happened, I'd share with the student how I sensed God's calling in my life, and then I'd give her Scriptures to read and compare. I wanted my students to understand both sides and figure out what God was trying to teach them through it all.

The Original Well-Worn Path

On this journey toward adulthood, we can guide students to well-worn paths of unmistakable truth and purpose. And then we can offer reminders along the way. One well-worn path that we can travel with students is deeply embedded in the history and experiences of people throughout Scripture. It begins early in the Old Testament, in Deuteronomy 6:4-9 (NLT):

> "Listen, O Israel! The LORD is our God, the LORD alone. And you must love the LORD your God with all your heart, all your soul, and all your strength. And you must commit yourselves wholeheartedly to these commands that I am giving you today. Repeat them again and again to your children. Talk about them when you are at home and when you are on the road, when you are going to bed and when you are getting up. Tie them to your hands and wear them on your forehead as reminders. Write them on the doorposts of your house and on your gates.

Another friend in ministry, Mike King, describes Deuteronomy as a pivotal book in the Old Testament. It connects the experiences of the Jewish people (before they understood who they truly were in God's eyes) with the stories of the redemptive nation they were to become. It details their journey in the wilderness as they prepared for the Promised Land. How fitting to find our guidance in leading students from the experiences of childhood, through the wilderness of adolescence, and into a promised land of maturity within the story of an ancient path of purposeful living!

Deuteronomy describes the well-worn path that—from the very beginning of God's covenant with the Jewish people—God encouraged them to travel over and over again with their children. It's an amazing picture of how we're to not only connect children to a collective spiritual heritage that links them to the people who've gone before them, but also keep them traveling toward their own spiritual identity.

Just like the Jewish people, we need external experiences and reminders to understand and reflect on the inward reality of God in our lives. We sometimes stand from afar as omniscient observers to the selfish ambitions, prideful actions, and dangerous choices of the Old Testament people. But in those moments, we're unknowing participants in the same story. Even though the scenery may look very different, the refrain of knowing God and needing him for our own shortcomings is no less significant for us than it was for the first people who heard God whisper to their hearts.

Deuteronomy 6:4-9 is the foundation on which Mile Markers is built. The Old Testament Law wasn't intended to be a list of negative commands, but rather a guide toward a life of wholeness and purpose so God's people could be blessed and then be a blessing to others. Each command grows out of and only makes sense in the context of the larger story that God is telling.

This part of the Law is described in terms of a journey of connection and legacy, while the Jewish people were actually watching their destiny unfold on a pilgrimage through the wilderness. The intent is to help young followers of God be connected to him and to all he has done, while living in the legacy of a people whose divine purpose was to usher in salvation to humanity. So what better rut to travel with our students than ancient words meant to bind the people's hearts to their Creator and offer them a Divine inheritance of purpose and belief.

BUILDING BRIDGES FOR PARENTS

Deuteronomy 6:4-9 reminds us of the beauty of God's plan, choosing parents' relationships with their children to be the central avenue of telling God's Story and passing on the legacy. There were no youth workers, coaches, or small group leaders in the wilderness with the Israelites; parents were the primary spiritual leaders, the teachers, and the mentors.

In the different cultural landscape we experience now, this passage still echoes God's plan. The difference is that sometimes we must play the role of a spiritual parent, and sometimes we need to encourage parents to play their spiritual role. Either way, these words can guide us in pointing students to the important mile markers of their lives, and they can also help us encourage parents to be leaders to their kids at a time when they're often discouraged in that role.

Mike King had two suggestions for helping parents take Deuteronomy 6:4-9 to heart.

1. A Scriptural Guide and Companion

Have you ever noticed a huge pendulum swing from the time when parents leave their first bundle of joy in the church nursery to when they're parenting a high schooler? When I dropped Lanie off at the church nursery those first few months, my "FYI" list for the nursery worker rivaled a college essay. I was sure this person would need a lot of help understanding my child in order to care for her. Lanie is in late grade school now, and I'm much more relaxed when I leave her in a teacher's or leader's care. This is partly because she can communicate her needs and ideas to them. And when she comes home, we're able to discuss and work through any problems or challenges she encountered.

But somewhere during middle school or the early high school years, students begin questioning their self-understanding, and at the same time they might stop turning to their parents as a primary source of guidance. That's when parents who feel they've lost their influence with their children are willing to follow the ideas of anyone who can reach their teenagers.

The hope for parents is that we can help them discover healthy ways to give their children freedom and gradually release them into more independence, while still walking with them on the journey toward adulthood. We can help parents apply this passage with their children—just like we do for our students. By providing ideas that encourage participation in their kids' lives and mapping out ways to help conversations with their children thrive, we offer a chance for the words of Deuteronomy 6 to become reality for families. When the relationship between parent and adolescent is strained, misunderstood, painful, or just plain struggling, these six verses offer parents a way of living alongside their children that might bridge some of the impasses in their relationship. These words can also challenge parents to look for moments to point the way to their kids every day.

2. A River of Guidance That Flows Naturally

The difficulty in guiding kids through their adolescent angst is that oftentimes the answers don't come quickly. Change comes gradually for students and their relationships. Even though an adolescent's desire to individuate may quickly show up in her behavior and attitudes over the course of a few months, the actual process of defining her identity apart from her parents takes much longer. So it takes a while for her to realize that becoming her own person doesn't mean completely severing the relationships and influence with her mom and dad. On the other hand, her abrupt about-face in how she talks to Mom or responds to Dad can cause her parents to panic and maybe even discourage her in the areas where she needs them to see past her words and intonation and gently guide her through the adolescent wilderness, not try to yank her out of it.

For several decades it seems that parents have been subtly and unintentionally encouraged to relinquish their spiritual influence to the church. But in the original story of God forming a body of believers, parents were God's choice to tell his Story. So we should help them do that as much as possible.

If we encourage dads and moms to take Deuteronomy 6:4-9 to heart; if we can help them to be intentional about faith and life conversations; if we can help them to be creative in seizing opportunities for memorable moments; and if we can help them experience the shalom (or peace) that God intended for our lives and relationships, then they'll encounter the moments when they can point the way or offer a valuable experience more often. Just as a river's natural path doesn't flow straight across a landscape but cuts back and forth and meanders at times, those moments between a parent and teenager may not come immediately. But they do come, and much more naturally over time.

Recognizing the Possibilities

A mile marker can be lots of things. It can be a planned event that builds an important memory, a surprise gift that reinforces a value or a message, a celebration for growth or accomplishment, a rescue from danger, a repeated experience that builds momentum, a sacrifice that changes priorities, an unexpected adventure, or a symbol that tells a story. Really, there are countless ways to use or create a mile marker moment. Many of them already exist in most youth ministries; they just might need more intention in their undertaking. Wherever a student may look back and see a significant place of growth or a pivotal moment of personal understanding, that's a possible mile marker.

Of course, there are already many occasions in students' lives that look like mile markers. Sometimes there's no need to reinvent the wheel but just to embrace an opportunity that already presents itself. Union and Jenks High Schools, two high schools in Tulsa, have such a celebrated rivalry that they've named their annual contest the "Backyard Bowl." It's a great high school sporting event, and ESPN even came out to film it in 2007. Students from each school create really catchy T-shirts; the super-fans come out painted from head to bellybutton (just the guys, of course!); and families from all over the city crowd into the bleachers of Chapman Stadium at the University of Tulsa. Even students who don't usually pay attention during football games can recite the highlights the next day. It's a night of competition and community at their best—not because both teams have so much talent but because of the spirit of the game. For the players from both schools, this game has a profound impact on their high school experience.

And it's a huge night for youth workers to enter the world of the players, cheerleaders, pom squads, band members, and student fans and cheer them all on. At such an event, we not only celebrate with them, but we also stay close enough to overhear the break-up between a guy and a girl or catch the rumor of where the post-game party is going to be and who'll be there. Youth workers can accomplish two things on a night like the Backyard Bowl: They show up at an event that's important to students, and they follow up when something goes wrong and a student needs help. No lesson is planned and no budget is necessary for this mile marker. But years later, students will remember it as one of the best or most impacting celebrations of high school. And they'll remember that you were there.

Looks Can Be Deceiving

But remember, too, some events just look like mile markers. They don't really stand up to the test of adding meaning and purpose to a student's adolescent journey. These include events such as prom, spring break trips, and a twenty-first birthday, for example. Let's call them "pseudo mile markers." Our society has inflated the significance of these kinds of events, and most often they're experienced in shallow ways that lack depth of purpose.

Prom may be a magnificent parade of sequined gowns, limousine rides, and high school revelry; but it's also quite possibly the absolute worst night for friendship tensions, irresponsible choices, and sexual regrets. Turning 21 may be the legal age to drink, but if 41 percent of eighth grade students and 62 percent of tenth graders say, "Been there, done that," then this celebration easily becomes just another night to drink way too much and ignore the nagging truth of possible alcoholism.[7] Finally, no one has to look very far in his or her community or the media to hear about a spring break trip to the beach that ended as a bad social experiment with consequences that will certainly echo into students' adult lives. Our students will continue embracing these moments as mile markers when we don't offer them anything with more substance.

Reclaim and Redeem

The good news is that none of these big moments are inherently bad. Our culture has just sold them as beautifully wrapped packages that are, in fact, empty. There's no reason why we can't reclaim important mile markers that have been robbed of their essence and redeem them for a greater good! For example, prom is usually one of the first times in students' lives that they stay out all night with the keys to the car and no curfew. When students leave the dance at midnight, they typically either go to an after-prom party or they rent a hotel room. Rarely does the after party have enough supervision, and sometimes parents rent the hotel rooms for their teenagers. There isn't a place in the universe where it's a good idea to rent a hotel room for students after the prom.

The point is that students might be given more responsibility and less accountability too quickly for this anticipated event. Think about it. On a Friday night, they have to be home by midnight, and their parents either wait up for them or lie in bed awake until they hear them come in. But on the very next night, the regular curfew is lifted, and all of the "checking in with Mom and Dad" steps are removed or diminished. Parents stay up for a while, but then they go to bed with their cell phone sitting on the nightstand, hoping to see their kids safe and sound at dawn. With a little rest ahead of time and some creative collaboration, we can help parents reclaim and redeem prom. The possibilities are endless! We shouldn't take it over. We need to help students celebrate a mile marker of more freedom. But we shouldn't completely disappear either. We should be standing on the sidelines with the parents and be invisible if students so wish; but by all means, adults should participate in this momentous night.

Creating a Deeper Well of Experiences

We aren't limited to just reclaiming and redeeming the pseudo mile markers in students' lives. We can also engage them in ways that stretch their abilities, test their perseverance, broaden their perspectives, and deepen their understanding. If her top 10 memories from the ages of 13 to 20 consist of her favorite episodes of *The Office,* all the clothes she bought on a vacation to Europe, and getting a sunflower tattoo on her ankle, then she's missed out on some wonderful life-defining experiences.

There's been a small but remarkable movement in some churches to incorporate a coming-of-age experience for guys in middle school or high school. These rite of passage events almost always include fathers or father figures in the guys' lives. I saw some real potential in this concept, so I asked my staff to gather a team of men and create a guys-only event that would focus on the intersection of their manhood, faith, and destiny. It's been a great success that gives fathers and important male role models a powerful setting for pouring into the lives of our young men.

Once we got that going, though, we realized we hadn't heard anything about such an experience for girls, except for the growing trend of purity banquets. I completely understand the great intentions of these occasions, and I applaud dads for initiating honest conversations with their daughters about sexual choices. However, while it's a night that may give dads the necessary support in expressing themselves to their daughters regarding a difficult subject, it also runs the risk of putting even more pressure and guilt on the girls in front of their peers. I'm not sure we should be making such a commitment easier for the parent and more difficult for the teenager. We should encourage dads to occasionally plan a father-daughter "date" where it's just the two of them having fun together, talking about his hopes for her life choices, and building her self-worth so she'll be more likely to embrace the values he's imparted to her.

Since we didn't know of any events for girls with the same purpose as our guys' rite of passage, a team of women began working on "Sweet 17," a weekend event during which we'd explore topics such as intimacy in relationships, living in a spiritual legacy, striving for wisdom, and healing for the wounds we often carry, among many other topics. The purpose was much the same as for the guys, just slanted for the way girls are typically wired. Moms and female mentors would all have a vital role during this retreat.

Other activities that might give our students a deeper well to draw from down the road are inviting students into experiences of giving and sacrificing for the sake of others that actually cost them something, confronting them with teachable moments about the slippery slide of dishonesty and cheating, equipping and training them to make wise financial choices, creating safe zones for dealing with family emotional baggage (most of us have some), and contemplating our personal decisions that have a global impact. Again, some topics may be pretty universal; others may be distinctive to a particular group or person.

MORE ROAD SIGNS

In considering what kinds of mile markers to use and when they're most effective, here are some practical reminders to post on our office walls or to keep flashing like neon signs in our brains.

Mile Markers by Inspiration, Not Imitation

Remember, the possibilities for different kinds of mile markers for students are unlimited. Kids are growing up in different places and with different experiences and influences competing for their attention. The sky is the limit, so work from inspiration. Don't limit your idea with imitation, which is just limitation without the L. Sure, we may read ideas online or in a book, or we may hear about something that we want our students to encounter. And that's great. There aren't many truly "new" ideas out there—just reinvented and repackaged ones. So that's what we should do—retool an idea to fit the kids we know, where we live, when it's most important for them, and in a way that speaks best to their experience.

Embrace the Sacred Messiness of the Journey

We should definitely plan for ministry, and then welcome the moments when a circumstance either forces a change in direction or completely obliterates our plan. Most youth workers either plan ahead and don't flex well when the plan has to change or they don't plan at all, which means chaos only increases with the addition of more uncertainty.

I call the journey toward adulthood "sacred messiness" because adolescents encounter unpredictable terrain on this road. But God is always working in them along the way. A helpful illustration might be a football game. The head coach is in charge of the game for his team, but he has assistant coaches spread out along the sidelines and possibly up in the booth. Each assistant coach leads a section of the team with a unique purpose in the game: Offense, defense, or special teams. The quarterback takes his cues from the offensive coordinator or head coach, but he can also call an audible on the line if necessary. When the ball snaps on a pass play, there is a plan; but influences from the other team's movements can change where the quarterback throws, which receivers get open, and how well the offensive line protects the quarterback. All of this affects how far the ball moves down the field. Sometimes the head coach tells everyone exactly what to do, and the team gives their best efforts to follow his directive. Ultimately, everyone's goal is to win the game, but afterward the game films might not resemble the game plan that was in place before the first kick-off.

Ministry is rarely neat and tidy every minute. If we try to control too much, we starve the spontaneity of God's Spirit and forget to listen for his whisper in the unexpected places. That's when we realize we have to call an audible or heed the call for a much needed Hail Mary play. If we never think ahead strategically, we aren't partnering with God as he coaches and inspires students to follow him.

To Stay on Course or Change Gears

I find this reminder really helpful for people who, like me, tend to switch things up almost impulsively. My boss once commented that sometimes I throw out an idea or program before I really give it a chance to catch on. So for me and other hyper leaders like me, it's so important to recognize when something works and keep using and improving it.

On the flip side, we shouldn't hold onto a plan just because it's as comfortable as an easy chair. When we forget why we do a certain event or project, it's time to change gears and breathe some life back into our journey with students. Leaders who love stability and repetition of a good thing need to periodically evaluate if a good idea has run its course or lost its essence.

EXIT RAMP

Adolescence has an ever-changing landscape whose beauty can awaken a student's soul one moment and whose destructiveness can wound her spirit the next. This road that our students are on is a long bridge to adulthood. They need guides to walk all the way across with them. And if we don't guide and encourage the real mile marker moments for students, they'll create or seek out their own. That's when they settle for pseudo mile markers that are cut and pasted throughout our society, and their adolescent years become a cookie-cutter experience that may taste good, but will never nourish their souls. Instead, let's lead them down well-worn paths that make them hungry for the Bread of Life.

1. Contemplate your own mile marker moments as an adolescent. How did they impact the direction of your life?

2. What are some pseudo mile markers that disappointed you?

3. What does the landscape of your student ministry look like? What are some specific mile markers that your students need?

4. Who can you invite to share the journey with students, so that no matter how many teenagers you reach, everyone is known, cared for, and safe?

5. Think of an event in your students' lives that's already a mile marker moment you can emphasize. Is there an event that can be reclaimed and redeemed? How?

6. List a few adjectives to describe the kind of well-worn path you'd like your students to come back to as adults.

The Journey Begins Here

*"Listen, O Israel! The LORD is
our God, the LORD alone."*
Deuteronomy 6:4 (NLT)

CHAPTER

4

In order to get driving directions from MapQuest, I have to enter a starting point. Once the addresses of the starting point and final destination are entered, the program provides a breakdown of the trip, including the mileage between turns and road changes. At the end of the report, there's a map that offers an overview of the entire trip. It also provides a link to get the directions in reverse, so I can navigate back to the starting place, if needed.

That's a picture of what we're doing to lead students down a road of personal and spiritual growth. We begin by giving them a place to start. Then we help them focus on the destination. Next, we break down that long journey into smaller distances with road signs and landmarks that keep them moving in the right direction. As often as possible, we refer them to Scripture as an overall map and guide for their journey. Lastly, we keep the reverse directions option very accessible in their lives so they can get back to the starting place if their journey should detour or if they lose their sense of direction.

The next few pages focus on the starting place—the beginning of the journey. When students begin their spiritual quest in the right place, the destination for their adolescent journey gradually comes into focus, too. According to Deuteronomy 6:4-9, personal understanding and purpose for any spiritual journey—including the adolescent pilgrimage—begin by understanding God and his purpose. When read alone, verse 4 seems to be an announcement: "Listen, O Israel! The LORD is our God, the LORD alone." But when it's read with the rest of the passage (through verse 9), it becomes the crucial reason why we should do all the things listed in these verses.

> Listen, O Israel! The LORD is our God, the LORD alone. And you must love the LORD your God with all your heart, all your soul, and all your strength. And you must commit yourselves wholeheartedly to these commands that I am giving you today. Repeat them again and again to your children. Talk about them when you are at home and when you are on the road, when you are going to bed and when you are getting up. Tie them to your hands and wear them on your forehead as reminders. Write them on the doorposts of your house and on your gates. (Deuteronomy 6:4-9, NLT)

Deuteronomy 6:4 is a one-sentence summary of faith that's recited by faithful Jewish believers each day. This verse highlights the crucial reason to look beyond ourselves to find our significance in God. But since it's an abstract concept to an adolescent ear, we have to begin this mile marker practice by paraphrasing it for their world. We need to make it a starting line they recognize. One way we can articulate that idea to students is by stating that life has purpose because God matters and our lives matter to him.

LISTEN FOR THE STORY OF PURPOSE

Just Shema

At a recent Young Life camp, I listened as hundreds of high school students from across the country bellowed the words to Taylor Swift's country hit "Our Song" during an evening club. I could tell by the volume and intensity of their voices that they didn't just know the song; they connected with its message. They sang it as though it was their song, or at least the words to a song they'd like to have written for them.

Music speaks to students that way. In the lyrics, the driving rhythms, and wailing instruments, they identify with the experience of the singer or the story she tells. And because teenagers listen to their favorite songs so often, the notes and lyrics become second nature to them.

Deuteronomy 6:4 is the beautiful, repetitive anthem that Jewish people still claim as their song, their story. When they first heard it, the people of Israel were waiting between the wilderness and the Promised Land. To help them understand their purpose, God gave them these words to write upon their hearts: "Listen, O Israel! The LORD is our God, the LORD alone." These are powerful words of connection and relationship to God. And before God challenges the Jewish people to love him, follow him, and tell his Story, he calls them to shema, or listen. Don't talk. No need for action yet. Just listen. Listen to the Story of God.

Listen to the refrain of God's creation: Raindrops, creaking trees, joyful birds, swirling desert winds, and mighty waterfalls. Listen to the many verses of all that God has done and all that he can do: Painted the sky, sculpted the landscape, rescued his beloved from slavery, divided a deep sea in half, and sent birds with food. Listen for God's voice: "Abraham, go to a foreign land and I will bless you. Jacob, you have wrestled with me, and I will never leave you. Joseph, your dreams will save your people. Moses, go back and I will do powerful things through you." Just listen. Listen and you'll recognize this Story and see God in it.

So before we ask students to make a decision about what they believe or to live their lives differently, we can compel them to just listen for a while. We can carve out moments in which there is no clever lesson or media-driven sermon. Even if we believe we're pretty effective at communicating God's Story, students still a need a chance to hear God's voice in their hearts, not just our voices clanging around in their heads. They need to hear God tell them the Story. When they know it well enough, it will leave an enduring imprint on their lives that they can claim as their own ballad of belief, rather than just an old song of hand-me-down faith that they don't know or understand.

Mile Marker This...

Throughout the remaining chapters of this book, you'll find "Mile Marker This..." sections that offer practical ideas that youth workers and parents can utilize as they journey alongside adolescents. (Some ideas will be unpacked further on the Mile Markers companion CD, including full instructions.)

MILE MARKER THIS...

No, Really...Just Listen

This practice helps students include listening in their definition of worship. Whether there's an entire hour of silence for high school students (work up to this one!) or two minutes of listening for sixth graders, students will slowly become more comfortable with the idea of listening for God in their lives. It's not an exercise in just being quiet. The goal is to help them actively listen for God's presence around them. Here are a few ways to begin—

- Read a Scripture passage
- Find a quiet place in a nature park
- Take a "no-talk" walk in the mountains

Mile Marker Keepsake

Early in your students' adolescence, or early in your relationships with teenagers, present them with some kind of mile marker journal or mile marker box to hold onto throughout their adolescent journey. This is a place where they can put lesson notes, prayer exercises, memory gifts, written thoughts, Scripture cards—you name it—anything they can come back to later. Make it earthy, rugged, and usable. Tell students at the beginning that over the next several years they'll experience many things that they'll want to remember, so they should use this keepsake to help them do just that.

Some students won't ever journal or keep things. But it's difficult to know who will actually use it and when, so give one to everyone you can. If you give a journal, make sure all of the journal sheets and lesson notes you hand out after that will easily fit into the journal so students will be more likely to use theirs.

Passing Period Prayers

Encourage adolescents to silently pray between classes and watch for God to show up in their day. Have them journal and share what they experienced or what God revealed to them as a result of praying and listening during some chaotic moments.

Imagine, Reread, and Repeat

Select a Scripture verse or passage and repeatedly weave it through a montage of photos that relate to its content. Let the words continue to fade and reappear on the screen in between pictures. The message on the screen should be the catalyst for God to speak to students' hearts. It can be introduced as the lesson for the day, and then leaders should step into the background and remain quiet. Or it can be used as a stand-alone prayer or worship experience in which youth are prepped before they enter. Adapt the length to fit the personalities and needs of the students. Close in silence with an AMEN on the screen. Don't sum it up, make announcements, or add anything afterward. Let God close this one with his own personal benediction for each student.

You Have Questions. God Has Answers.

Students can write a question for God in their journals, next to a Scripture passage in their Bibles, or on a piece of paper posted where they'll see it throughout the day. Encourage them to refer to it often and pray for deeper understanding. When they sense God has either answered the question or given them insight into the issue, they should write the answer next to the question and date it. Point out that God might use another Scripture passage, a person, or a circumstance to add to their understanding.

Sacred Spaces

Adolescent lives are so busy. Start off the school year or a new season in the ministry calendar by challenging students to set aside sacred space in their lives. It can be a time, or a place, or both. It can be repetitive or varied. Offer an illustration of how to avoid squeezing God out of our schedules. I like to use the baseball and rice demonstration that I learned from my friend Martha King. Put a baseball inside a clear glass jar and pour dried rice over it until the jar is completely full. Show students that the lid will go on the jar. Then empty all of the contents of the jar and repeat the exercise. But this time, put the rice in first. Students will see that the baseball no longer fits if all of the little pieces are poured in first. Next, explain how it's the same with our daily lives: If we pour all of the little pieces of activity and commitments into our days first, then there's no space left to fit in the big, sacred, sustaining presence of God. One great way to use this practice is to help parents teach and model this lesson by creating sacred space in their family life.

NOT JUST A STORY FOR ANYONE, BUT SOMEONE

When I watch a movie, I find I'm catapulted out of my seat, outside the theater, and into the life of the story being told. Maybe it's the house-sized screen, the stadium seating, the surround sound, or the larger-than-life characters. But whatever it is, it's almost as if the story were written so I could enter into it. In a very surreal way, I feel as though I've known the surroundings, the plot, and the characters all along. More than once, after witnessing a powerful cinematic experience, I've walked out into the reality of daylight and had to remind myself that the parking lot, my car, and the hot sun were the real story, while the story I'd just exited was an ingeniously crafted work of fiction.

The Story God tells in Scripture isn't meant for a random, haphazard listener. God doesn't tell it and hope some passerby will politely stop and join his story-time circle. It's an epic narrative dedicated to the people whom God chose to work in and through to demonstrate his grace and truth to the world. God had the Israelites in mind all along to lead the cast of this drama. God is the Author, and he surrounds the Jewish people with a compelling saga that invites them to join in so that many generations of humanity beyond their relatively small tribal life will also hear the Story. And by then the Story will have the biographies of these first actors and their children's children added into the credits.

Way of Walking

The wonderful difference between my movie experiences and the Story of God is that his Story is the real stuff of life, not just well-crafted imagination. When we encourage students to listen to the Story, they'll feel an invitation to make it their way of walking. They'll be drawn to listen to the refrain of God's truth so often that it not only becomes intertwined with their identity, but also draws them into the Story as participants. When they see the Story of God as a story meant for them and with parts written for them, they'll begin to glimpse a greater good for their lives that reaches back into history and connects them to a path rich with the chapters of God's work in human lives.

MILE MARKER THIS...

Family Shema

Instead of telling her kids to be careful or behave every time they walked out the door, one mom I know offered her children this powerful reminder, "Remember who you are and whose you are...." That pretty much sums up Deuteronomy 6:4-9! Give your students or their parents a chance to imagine what they could regularly say to each other as a reminder of their spiritual identity and purpose.

Make It a Movie Night

This isn't an aimless entertainment option but a cinematic launching pad for discussion and sharing. It gives youth workers, parents, and students a familiar entertainment medium to experience together, and then it sets the tone for good conversation afterward. Picking movies with spiritual substance is the key. They can be powerful and moving, such as *Amazing Grace*, *The Passion of the Christ*, and the *Lord of the Rings* trilogy. They can also portray honest struggle, such as *The Shawshank Redemption* or *Schindler's List*. Or how about a movie that asks lots of questions about our humanity, spiritual forces, or life after death, such as *The Sixth Sense*, *The Matrix*, and *The Exorcism of Emily Rose*. Finally, adolescents will always remember when we're willing to watch a movie for the sake of understanding something we don't necessarily agree with, such as *The Da Vinci Code*.

Book Club

Some students would gain a lot from being a part of a book community that reads and discusses the works of great Christian voices, historical and modern. *Mere Christianity* by C. S. Lewis, *Confessions* by St. Augustine, or *The Cost of Discipleship* by Dietrich Bonhoeffer are just a few deep-read suggestions of voices from the past that still speak volumes into our lives today.

Blue Like Jazz by Donald Miller, *Velvet Elvis* by Rob Bell, and *Letters from a Skeptic* by Gregory and Edward Boyd are examples of emerging thought in Christian writing that may resonate with teenagers as they seek to understand who Jesus was and is and what that means to their faith. For students who aren't yet interested or ready for the themes of these books, there are other great books, such as *Be the Change* by Zach Hunter, *Don't Buy the Lie* by Mark Matlock, or *The Case for Christ* (student edition) by Lee Strobel and Jane Vogel.

Bible Biographies
Help students experience the lives of biblical people by writing or finding biographies that interpret their stories with relevance and imagination. Either *The Book of God: The Bible as a Novel* by Walter Wangerin Jr. or *The Message* by Eugene Peterson is a great place to start. Read these books to students out loud during lessons or devotions, or incorporate them into a personal devotional experience.

GOD MATTERS IN STUDENTS' LIVES

Not a God, but the Lord God
I remember first studying Greek and Roman mythology in a junior high language arts class. As a young believer, my first impressions of these stories about deities who ruled the world from Mount Olympus was that the gods were magnificent, powerful, vindictive, and silly all at the same time. Although the myths we read in class certainly had something to teach about living life, the lessons were usually being taught by the humans and learned by the deities. The gods seemed so wrapped up in their own wants and mishaps that they couldn't possibly impact humanity too much for the good. Humans prayed and sought the assistance of the gods, but they were often on their own to find resolution.

I frequently hear people assign some of the same characteristics to God that are portrayed in these stories of the Greek and Roman gods of antiquity. Maybe in their understandable frustration over events in their own lives, or in an honest search to understand the faltering of our world, they picture God much like a mythological creature who is too wrapped up in himself to do much for us. But the Story of God is about One who is time and again speaking, intervening, teaching, warning, helping, healing, sacrificing, listening, loving, waiting, judging, and guiding in the lives of people.

The certainty in Deuteronomy 6:4 is that God proclaimed himself the Lord to the Jewish people—not one of many mythological characters struggling with inconsistent values and moral waverings. God's presence in their lives—and ours—isn't just a hope or a possibility or even an accident. God is the initiator of life and breath. He's the reason we wake up and breathe every day. God matters in students' lives because he's the one who gave them lives to live, and God is paying attention to each moment of their journeys. God isn't too busy, too self-consumed, or too frivolous with his supernatural existence. God's actions are trustworthy, his character doesn't change, and he's intricately participating in human destiny. God isn't just any god. He is the God.

Unrivaled Deity

Another huge struggle for people throughout the stories of Scripture was a world of pluralism. Not only were there incongruities in describing God's character, but there were also multiple deities to worship—man-made idols that were somehow supposed to bring meaning to life, as well as natural wonders of creation being assigned divine characteristics.

The time in the wilderness was no different for the Jewish people. They'd spent 400 years—at least six generations of their ancestry—entrenched in the religious pluralism of ancient Egyptian culture. That was a long time to stay focused on the God of their fathers, whom they couldn't see, when they were surrounded by visible, tangible representations of lesser gods. So when God rescued them, he made it clear to those he delivered—and to their captors—that he's the unrivaled Deity.

Through the plagues and miracles of the exodus, God demonstrated that his power should be trusted and feared. He alone can interrupt nature. He alone can give and take life. He alone is able to protect those he loves and deliver justice for his injured people. Nothing that the Israelites left behind in Egypt, nothing they discovered in the wilderness where they wandered for 40 years, and nothing they would eventually find in the Promised Land could compete with the character of God. The unmistakable truth that God alone was Creator of all and King of their lives was the beginning of their understanding about who they were and what their purpose would be.

Our students may not be tempted to put their hope in a carved statue or the sun, but they'll be presented with many worldviews and perspectives about the meaning of life. They'll be encouraged to trust in only the things they can see, or in mystical experiences that are no more enduring than vapors of incense. Culture offers them well-adorned replacements to faith and obedience, and sometimes we feel as though our small, insignificant efforts to put God's Story up in lights will never be able to compete with the initial brilliance of an alluring distraction.

But we must remember that the Story we tell isn't powerful because of how we tell it; it's transformative because it's true and teenagers' hearts resonate with truth. They'll be told it doesn't matter what they believe in or that there are many ways to God. They need reminders, evidence, and experiences that point to God—the only God who matters. They need to know they can trust God with their lives and that nothing is stronger than God. They need to have confidence that God is the Author and Giver of all that is good and all that is true, whenever and wherever they encounter goodness and truth.

MILE MARKER THIS...

Truth Testing

Give students the opportunity to examine ideas, promotions, and belief systems in their world and see if they stand up to the test of truth in Scripture. For example, ABC Family is an entire channel of ideas and propositions about what the American family has become. Even their tagline, "A new kind of family," has a wealth of commentary to unpack. Students can look at the premise for ABC Family's various shows and advertisements and have hundreds of ready-made discussions about what ABC means by this "new family" they're talking about.

You should decide ahead of time on a list of items to test or let students come up with their own. Then provide a list of Scriptures they can search, people they can interview, and Web sites or books they can refer to to discover if the idea promoted in culture is really true. Give them a chance to journal or share what they learned with you and their peers. Students can even look for songs, movies, or quotes that relate to the topic and share why they're relevant or irrelevant. Allow time for discussion and debriefing since it's possible that some answers will cause disagreement or lead to more questions. Both circumstances can truly engrave a lasting reminder of testing for truth if topics are given ample foundation in Scripture and treated with integrity.

Take on Culture One Untruth at a Time

Your students (and even some adults) may not know who Bill O'Reilly is or agree with his views, but the title of one of his recent books, *Culture Warrior,* captures the idea of not blindly embracing everything that culture says is important or true. Teenagers can be culture warriors in their faith and find ways to live counter to untruth. Help them examine the things in their lives that are considered very true or very important, such as "It's impossible to remain a virgin until you get married" or "Everyone cheats a little" or "The greatest senior trips are partying on the beach in exotic places." When they come up with one or more issues that need a countercultural challenge in their lives, encourage them to create or follow a plan that's more true and more meaningful to them. Younger teens might need more adult help to identify untruth and implement a concrete plan.

Idol Check

Walk students through an exercise of checking the "idols" in their lives. First, incorporate a personal reflection in a lesson or message that describes the different kinds of idols found in Scripture and how they affected people's faith. Then give students a list of possible distractions and distortions that might be receiving their wholehearted commitment today in place of their devotion to God. The list can include sports, fashion, image, material possessions, boyfriend, girlfriend, greed, friendships, success, and more.

THEIR LIVES MATTER TO GOD

My youth pastor, Jeff Mugford, had a signature benediction. I often heard him say, "You matter to me, and you matter to God." Whether he was closing a letter or saying good-bye, his final thought was usually this summary of care and connection. These words were always reinforced with actions that communicated the same message. When I played basketball on the second string of the B team for East Junior High, he came to watch me play. As an avid basketball enthusiast, I'm sure he cringed at my lack of skill, but he never let it show. He just cheered me on for the entire three minutes that I played in the game.

Later in junior high, Jeff asked me to sing at his ordination service. That one really surprised me, because although singing was the most important activity in my life at the time, there were plenty of other students in Jeff's ministry who were better, more experienced singers. Knowing he chose me instead of an adult or a more talented student was a mile marker moment for me because that choice went beyond what he saw as my ability to a deeper reality of a young fragile faith.

I was an adolescent girl struggling to like what I saw in the mirror. I was also an enthusiastic young believer who needed the seeds of leadership to be nurtured in my life by using my gifts in a positive way. I was on a journey in the adolescent wilderness, where one day my focus was on my natural strength as a singer, and the next day I couldn't see anything strong or beautiful in the mirror's reflection. Jeff's simple request for me to sing reverberated with the truth that my little dream of singing professionally someday mattered to him and it mattered to God—even if life eventually took me in a different direction. Jeff didn't give me a pep talk about the realities of making it in the music business or even offer the heart-to-heart conversation about me being good but not great. He never discouraged me. As you can guess, that experience didn't launch my music career, but it did propel my heart closer to God.

We've all heard the phrase "Jesus with skin on" when referring to a person who lives out the incarnation of Christ in our lives. To me, that's the echo of "The LORD is our God" in Deuteronomy 6:4. Not only is he the God, but he's also our God—a relationship that's shared between God and me, between you and me, and between God and us. It's personal and it's corporate. As my friend Joyce McCormick likes to explain, our horizontal relationships with others should be reflections of our vertical relationship with God. It's that life-giving reality that each of us matters to God right down to our innocent, youthful dreams, and God calls us to be devoted to one another in the same way as we walk through life together.

No spiritual journey is meant to be taken alone. So in youth ministry, it's also a shared journey, even when we aren't walking right in step with our students. When we share the journey with them, they also see God walking with them. God enters into unexpected places like their doubt and pain. God is there in a high school hallway filled with students who desperately need to understand their purpose. God maneuvers in and out of the middle school cafeteria where most are wondering if they're invisible to the world. God is there in that discomfort because those kids matter to him. When they understand that core truth, they see that their life matters and so does this adolescent pilgrimage.

MILE MARKER THIS...

Connection Time

Every Wednesday for almost five years, I enjoyed the company of five to six girls who invaded my office right after school. Sometimes we just sat around and talked, sometimes they talked me into buying them food, and always we just shared time and space together. It wasn't a Bible study or organized small group, but it was a weekly connection time for my heart and theirs. Each of those girls would now say that those Wednesdays when we spontaneously made up the plan as we felt inspired were some of their most cherished memories in Redeemer's student ministry. And I can certainly say the same for me! Those days prepared their hearts to be aware of God's goodness and movement in their lives in the moments outside of our time together.

Adolescents need meaningful time with parents and adults where the agenda is them, the lesson is whatever silly or serious questions are burning on their hearts at the moment, and the only plan is to enjoy the connection. Go get coffee, window shop, play Frisbee golf, or drive a scenic route and use those activities as avenues to conversation. There are plenty of students out there who cannot name one adult who has unstructured time available for them to just sit and be together. But for those who do have that outlet, theirs is often a stronger, more amazing faith journey.

Onsite Lunch Appearances

For the parent or youth worker who can get away during lunch, it's a great thing to just show up on campus with a student's favorite fast-food meal and maybe a few extras for their friends. If this is a new practice and he's feeling a bit awkward about your presence, you can quickly adapt the plan and say you were just bringing a surprise delivery. He'll still know and remember that you thought of him and showed up.

Surprise Invite

Invite a teen or tween to meet you somewhere fun or symbolic for some "you matter to me" time. Use a creative delivery method, such as a message inside a balloon that says Pop Me or a note on a cookie bouquet. Youth workers can invite parents to help with transportation for pre-drivers or suggest their older teenagers' favorite places to meet. Parents can leave an invitation on a pillow, the bathroom mirror, or even the car's steering wheel. The destination should be an activity or backdrop for quality time. You can have a picnic of her favorite foods, bring a present or book to give to her, or plan an adventure that the two of you can conquer together. Just make it an event in which she'll be reminded that she matters to you in a big way.

HELPING PARENTS BUILD BRIDGES

Keeping in mind that the passage in Deuteronomy 6 is actually speaking to parents, how do we help them find a place of spiritual influence in their kids' lives? We live in a world in which so many voices speak into students' lives that parents often feel their own voices are being drowned out by all of the noise. What encouragement can we offer in parent meetings and through personal encounters that will inspire them to hang in there?

I've found that parents either share their own faith experiences easily with their kids, or they struggle to find the words for those all-important conversations. There are a lot of understandable reasons why a parent might be comfortable in a spiritual influence role or shy away from it. If a mom has contemplated her own walk with God, she may understand that when she's talking to her daughter about spiritual topics, she can't step into the authoritative role that comes with the "mom" territory. Rather, she must remain in the influencing role and play the part of a friend who's on the same journey. Thus, she probably feels pretty comfortable coaching her daughter's faith. On the other hand, it's possible for a father with a newfound faith to feel ill-equipped to lead spiritually in his kid's life. This could be because he might feel as though he knows too little about his faith, or worry that inconsistencies in his own life might short-circuit his leadership.

There are parents with a deep and abiding faith who by all accounts cannot step into their child's spiritual journey. I don't know why, exactly. But one guess is that it's because faith is a very personal, intimate topic and sharing what they believe is like unclothing their spiritual selves. Another reason might be that all through grade school many of our children receive their spiritual foundation in Sunday school classes and Vacation Bible School. So parents may unintentionally let church become the default resource for those conversations. Then years down the road when they realize their child needs more guidance than one youth leader can offer, those conversations feel awkward and inhibited.

It's important to remember that parents who have their own spiritual wrestlings or agnostic leanings can fit into one of those two groups, too.

I know parents who don't share their stories with their kids because they have so many doubts. I also have friends who've resolved that they can live with the uncertainty in their hearts, and they articulate that reality to their children in an honest way. Nevertheless, youth workers still have an important encouraging role to play with these parents. It's very possible that a parent who's paralyzed by doubts needs a sounding board for their questions. It's a beautiful picture to consider: Instead of jumping in alongside a student's spiritual pilgrimage, a youth worker might come alongside a struggling parent and guide him in a way that allows him to eventually walk in tandem with his son. And as I've learned from my own friends, walking in step with a parent who is a thoughtful, nontraditional believer is good for all of us.

I recently asked a lifelong friend of mine if I could someday tell his story, along with the stories of other people I've known who don't embrace the entirety of Christianity. He agreed but added with gentle sarcasm that he "would be my little project, but he would not be a star pupil." That conversation rattled me a little because it dawned on me that after years of friendship, he might just believe that he'd been my spiritual project all along. What I failed to communicate was how much he'd taught me about asking hard questions and how much I'd learned about getting off the Christian platform and talking about my faith in an authentic way. I know he has those honest conversations with his own daughters and encourages them to decide for themselves.

Wherever parents are on their own spiritual quests and whatever assuredness or doubts they live with, we still have much to offer and receive in those relationships. And whatever is shared during honest exchanges and respectful conversations can only deepen the imprint of faith on their kids' hearts. With that in mind, make it a practice to know the parents of your students as much as possible. Meet them for lunch or coffee and ask them to tell their stories. Ask for their input about their kids' needs and their insights into the teen culture they've observed. Ask them how the church is doing in offering community and direction for them or their kids. We won't always get the answer we want or expect, but any story or response from a parent will add to the depth of our understanding about their family and their kids—and it may just edify our own prejudices or assumptions for the good.

Here are a few helpful encouragements to give to parents when they're leading their kids.

Spiritual Giants Need Not Apply

During one short season of my daughter's second-grade year, she was quite lonely because of the natural flow of grade school friendships. I offered to be the stand-in friend when she needed a buddy to play with, and she explained why she couldn't accept my offer: "Thanks, Mom. But when adults play and pretend to lose a game or be bad at something, it's not as much fun because I know they can really do better than I can."

Conviction showered down on me, but not because I'm probably better than she is at a lot of activities (purely because of my age and experience). No, in that moment I was challenged by the fact that Lanie doesn't need me to pretend to be bad at things I'm good at; she needs to see me struggle and work hard on things that are difficult for me. If she sees that I don't have it all together, then she'll be less afraid to fail at something like dribbling a basketball or maybe even following God. We need to passionately reiterate to parents that they don't have to be spiritual giants. Students will be intimidated if they see their parents as people who never struggle, but they'll identify with their parents if they see them working through the struggles.

Parents Don't Have to Know It All

I have an answer for everything. Really. It may not be the right answer, but before another person's question or concern is fully articulated to me, my overzealous brain commentator is already forming a response. That ability probably comes in handy during obnoxious debates, but it's not too helpful when my intent is to guide a conversation instead of take it hostage. Nor is having all the answers a prerequisite for parents to talk to their teenagers about life and faith. Sometimes parents avoid the conversation because they know they don't have all the answers to the questions that might come up. So they need our encouragement not to steer away from difficult topics. Kids don't need their parents to be the source of all answers, but they do need them to be a source of safe inquiry.

Offer parents these two helps. First, students don't always ask a question in order to get the answer. They may just need a sounding board to help them figure out their own answers or affirm their conclusions. They might also be okay with not getting an immediate answer, because as maturing people they're wise enough to know that not all answers come quickly or easily. Second, everyone can benefit by searching for the answer together. If a student knows his dad is honest enough to say, "I don't know the answer," and interested enough to help him look for it, then that dad's influence quotient just shot up several notches.

Parents Need to Be on Their Own Honest Spiritual Quest

I believe that one of the biggest mistakes any of us could make is to live as if our quest for spiritual answers is complete. Although I put my hope and trust in God's Story, there is no way—even with Scripture studies or advanced seminary degrees—to reconcile every spiritual question that arises. Paul confesses this reality as he writes to the church in Corinth. He looks around and considers all of the wisdom that God has given the young church through his remarkable life, and Paul's conclusion is that everything we know and experience now is only a poor reflection in a mirror, only part of what we'll fully know someday (1 Corinthians 13:12). So one of the best gifts we can give to parents is to humbly model a life of continued growth and to encourage them to keep searching for themselves, even if they're doubters or novices. Just because someone seems to have made up her mind not to believe, that doesn't mean God won't someday convince her otherwise! And I've found that students who have honest and open dialogue with their parents about faith, regardless of their beliefs, are more likely to own their own faith more quickly because they were given room to make a decision for themselves.

Another consequence of adults not pursuing their own spiritual growth is that kids look at our ho-hum approach to faith and wonder if they'll be the same way someday. They're going to naturally gravitate to adults whose faith is vibrant and dynamic because in those individuals' lives, students see a desirable destination that they'd like to travel to themselves.

MILE MARKER THIS...

The Parent Chat

Organize a literal or virtual chat room where parents can meet together in real life or online and find resources for leading and teaching their children. Provide resources, links, and materials to help them stay informed about youth culture, as well as suggestions for how to help their child walk the adolescent journey. Let them know they can lean on each other for advice and support, but you're also there to strengthen their relationships with their children. Caution them not to use the venue for "discussing" each other's kids—that will backfire in a heartbeat.

Parent Ministry 101

Part of youth ministry is walking alongside families. Communication and understanding between youth workers and parents is strengthened when we spend a little time together apart from adolescents. So organize parent lunches that they can fit in during a workday or meet them for coffee—just to hear their stories and get to know them better. Those small efforts will build trust for partnering to lead their kids. When a youth worker senses she'll lose authenticity with a student if she spends time with that student's parent, she can coordinate another staff member or youth leader to be a source of encouragement and a resource for that parent.

EXIT RAMP

On a family vacation several years ago, Gary asked me to print out the directions to our destination from MapQuest. He's the trip organizer in our family, but I was glad to help. So on the day we were to leave, while Gary was still at work, I went online and entered the starting and ending locations. The directions came up easily, with no address glitches or computer quirks. So I printed them out and put them with the atlas and travel guides.

Our travel to our destination was easy—and just as MapQuest had outlined it. But we encountered a different story coming home. At the moment we realized we were lost, Gary asked, "Did you print out the reverse directions?" This question sums up our organizational styles pretty well. Gary is the detailed, list-checking, get-the-reverse-directions kind of person. I'm the big picture, hope I remember the list, don't-get-the-reverse-directions kind of person. So, no, I didn't get the reverse directions, and we quickly realized we couldn't travel on the same routes we'd used the first time. We'd have to figure out a new path to get back home.

The point of helping students start their spiritual journeys in the right place is to provide them with an anchor point. When life gets hard—a friend dies, family life implodes, school is distressing, a date turns into assault, or a party gets out of hand—their journey may forever be impacted in a way that alters the road on which they're traveling. They might need a set of reverse directions because they can't get back home the same way they came. That road is now blocked or impossible to travel.

The kinds of mile markers that emphasize starting with God and who God is are the "reverse directions." They're the events that students remember at crucial moments to get them back to a place where they can start over. They're the foundational truths that will light the way whenever they encounter dark moments in life.

1. Why is it so hard to just listen?

2. Share or contemplate what the Jewish Shema means to you.

3. When did God's Story first seem real and personal to you?

4. How can we help adolescents understand how much they matter to God?

First I Am a Traveler, Then a Guide

*"And you must love the L*ORD *your God with all your heart, all your soul, and all your strength. And you must commit yourselves wholeheartedly to these commands that I am giving you today."*
Deuteronomy 6:5-6 (NLT)

CHAPTER

5

Early in my daughter Lanie's second grade year, our family traveled to Tahlequah, Oklahoma, to the Cherokee Heritage Center. Outside the museum, we meandered around a circular path of buildings and exhibits meant to imitate the layout of a precolonial Cherokee village. Our guide, Geanna, who very much looked the part of an ancient Cherokee woman, led us around the path and talked to us for more than an hour. She gave us a glimpse of Cherokee life 700 years ago by explaining the craftsmanship of a dugout canoe, demonstrating toolmaking, describing sacred rituals, and telling us the stories of Cherokee values. She'd walked the path of the stories many times, and thus she could guide us and answer our questions because the ancient history of her ancestors had become intertwined with her own story. It seemed Geanna's entire life was shaped by her work at the Heritage Center. I couldn't imagine her turning off this story that was so intricately woven into her identity. She understood more of her own story because she knew the story of the ancient Cherokee people.

Wouldn't youth ministry be so much easier if we could take our students to walk a real-life ancient path in an actual geographical location to nurture their own spiritual identity? By seeing the world in which the stories began and touching the enduring artifacts of an era gone by, they might feel strengthened in their belief. But even though those tangible reminders at the Heritage Center were powerful, our family didn't feel the ethos of ancient Cherokee life because we visited the village. We found it fascinating because our guide shared her part in a greater story on a journey that she'd claimed as her own.

As intriguing and moving as the stories of biological ancestry are, the story we want to tell our students is an even more incredible narrative because it's a saga of spiritual ancestry. It's the story of God's work in and through people since the first day of creation. Yet those of us in ministry can unintentionally turn off the story in our own lives when we aren't telling it to students. We can explain the plot, recite pivotal quotes, and dramatize the climax; but our lives outside of ministry are often separate from the story we tell. We share the story as if we're the tour guides and not a part of the story. We encourage students to travel a road upon which we've become stranded.

THE "YOUS" COME BEFORE THE "THEMS"

It's crucial for us to walk the walk that our students hear us talk about so much. Not only do we have to be familiar with the road that we're asking students to travel, but we must also be travelers on the same road. In meditating on verses 5 and 6 of Deuteronomy chapter 6, it struck me how the author doesn't mention "them"—the children who are the intended recipients of this spiritual legacy that the Jewish parents are to carry. These two sentences are talking to the adults—you and me, the leaders and guides. It's not until verse 7 that we get directions regarding how to pass this destiny on to our kids.

Contrast my family's tour guide experience at the Heritage Center with the tour guide character that Bonnie Hunt plays in the 1993 movie Dave (in which Kevin Kline plays a presidential look-alike). As she leads visitors through the hallowed halls of the White House, she's constantly repeating, "We're walking; we're walking," to her tour group, even when someone has a question or wants her to elaborate on something. It's a funny little comedic insert into the storyline, but she's basically a tour guide who seems disengaged with telling the story of the White House and weary of the whole ordeal. It's not a special story to her anymore, even though the people in her tour groups are enthusiastic and riveted by everything she tells them.

We need to take time to tend to our own spiritual journey. We should be conscious of seasons in our lives when we might as well be saying, "We're walking; we're walking," because it's obvious that our journey with God has lost some of its essence. It doesn't happen to everyone the same way. One day, it's because we've overbooked our lives with too many events, or we're trying to personally reach too many students on our own, leaving us emotionally and spiritually spent with no downtime left to recharge.

Another day, it might simply be the difficulties of ministry, which often stem from working with people who are just like us—flawed and in need of God's continued redemption in their lives. These difficulties are a familiar chorus of unrealistic expectations of church staff and misplaced priorities in the church vision: More counting the people in the seats than hearing their life-changing stories; staff dress codes that improve our look but not our ministry to students; rules and unspoken "no-nos" that keep the kids who need to hear about God's love the most on the outside looking in; and greater importance given to the presentation of our message, rather than trusting its simplicity and power to transform lives without slick marketing and trendy programs.

Then there are the days when we're walking through our own pain and find ourselves in a place with more questions than answers. Marital stress, secret struggles, broken histories that seem to follow us—all of these can rob us of the joy of our own salvation. Even though it's hard to let these days that strain our endurance become front and center on our radar, we must resist pushing them aside in an effort to be the strong leader. Students are watching how we live, how we make choices, and how we deal with pain. They need us to let down our guard and courageously face our own struggles. Otherwise, they won't have a spiritual mentor; they'll just have a tour guide.

Reflect on Our Own Spiritual Journeys First

When my son Garrison was born, I stepped out of full-time ministry for a season. At first my catchy little response to people who asked why I'd left an amazing youth ministry position after 13 years was, "I need to tend to my growing youth ministry at home!" Although I do believe God nudged me to take a sabbatical from full-time staff ministry until both of my children are in school, I now understand more fully that God also took me out for the sake of my own spiritual identity. I didn't fully grasp the depth of my circumstance until about a year later, but gradually the condition of my spiritual journey came into focus.

The recognition began when I ran into Craig Groeschel one Sunday on a LifeChurch.tv campus. He's the senior pastor of a multi-site church, so he doesn't know me that well. But he asked a question that penetrated my soul: "So now that you aren't doing ministry all the time, are you having an identity crisis?" Ding ding ding! The bell went off in my brain. He nailed it. Within just a few sentences in our conversation, Craig zeroed in on my spiritual journey and he didn't even know it! That morning began my cognitive recognition of being a 36-year-old woman, the wife of Gary, and the mother of Lanie and Garrison, who'd forgotten what it was to follow Christ without leading a ministry.

But that was only my analytical response. It took my heart another six months to catch up with the facts. By that time every day seemed to be a reminder that ministry life had moved on without me. Why did I even need a cell phone or a text-messaging package anymore? It rarely rang, and the text messages were few and far between. My life no longer had the natural intersections at church and at school with those students I'd cared for, so our connections just didn't happen very often. My friends in ministry were still doing ministry; so their lives were full, and they didn't know my situation to check in on me. I blocked out three to five hours a week to engage in ministry of some kind. But soon I realized that Garrison was not ready for this and would just cry the entire time I was gone.

I felt desperate. I'd been stripped of an identity that I'd cherished. Finally, I collapsed in tears one day as Garrison slept peacefully down the hall. Admittedly, when I read my Bible I don't usually expect that the page I open to will address what I am going through at that moment. But right then, God met me in my moment of sorrow with the words of Psalm 42:4-6a (NLT).

> My heart is breaking as I remember how it used to be: I walked among the crowds of worshipers, leading a great procession in the house of God, singing for joy and giving thanks amid the sound of great celebration! Why am I discouraged? Why is my heart so sad? I will put my hope in God! I will praise him again—my Savior and my God!

It took me many weeks to begin working through the messiness and depression that I'd finally recognized in my soul. I'd led a great procession of students and families into a life of knowing God—and I really missed it. But when I closed my Bible on that day of reckoning, I understood two things very clearly. First, my heart was breaking because I'd allowed the beautiful privilege of leading students to Christ to outshine the beauty of putting my hope in God. I knew I needed to figure out how to be a follower again, and God had given me a tremendous season of life to do just that. Second, I felt not only God's assurance that he did have more ministry planned for my journey, but also his conviction that the opportunity to love my spouse more fully and cherish my children without feeling torn between them and the needs of others was a gift I needed to finally open and enjoy.

Taking stock of our own spiritual condition is so important to our ministries. Paying attention to where we are on our journey with God certainly affects how and where we lead students. And understanding that yes, God does call us into the ministry places we enter, but sometimes God also calls us back. God may call us to retreat so he can better equip us. God desires for us to relinquish our wants so he can redeem them to meet our needs. God also calls us to remember where we began, what he's done, and all that he's promised us, so we'll be renewed and ready to lead others down the road.

Examine the Power of Our Own Adolescent Mile Markers

Whenever I train new student ministry volunteers, I always ask them to come to the meeting with a picture from their adolescence and an embarrassing story from those years. Before a new leader ever spends time with kids, I want to know if they can remember an unskewed inkling of their own adolescent journey. Even if adolescence in the twenty-first century looks different from 50 years ago, the season between childhood and adulthood has never been a cakewalk for any of us.

After all of the volunteers share their stories and pictures, I contribute my own teenage humiliations. I project my teenage picture up on the big screen. It's one of me sitting on my bed and doing homework in eighth or ninth grade, which sounds generic enough. The "Oh mys" come when people look at my clothing and face. I made the outfit, which was a bright melon-colored shirt with large white buttons on the sleeves and pants with one-inch wide teal, melon, white, and seafoam green vertical stripes. The look was completed with permed, chin-length hair and round, thick glasses. The story I usually tell is about being asked to my senior prom through a note that read, "Will you go to prom with me?" and had a box to check for yes, no, and maybe. I checked no.

This little warm-up exercise is fun but also very purposeful. After the group has sufficiently laughed at and with one another, we share the more meaningful moments of adolescence that helped shape the person that each of us has become. We talk about our own mile marker experiences. We share about how a person left an imprint on our lives. We reminisce about the events that reshaped us. We talk about the things that still anchor our faith today. For me, the highlights are my parents investing their time, finances, and care into the lives of foster children; my youth minister listening to every word I said and believing in me beyond my adolescent awkwardness; and the difficulties and opportunities of moving twice during high school.

There are places that stand out on the horizon of our own spiritual journeys whenever we look back into our lives. These are the mile markers we should contemplate for the sake of clarity in our own lives and personal missions, but also for the sake of helping our students experience their own mile markers, too. It's healthy for students to hear that even though we're model material now (yeah, right), we didn't have the greatest fashion sense then. It's also good for them to hear how we snorted when we laughed (and still do!), took a trip that changed us, read a Scripture that made us really contemplate God's work in our lives, and found a friendship in an unlikely peer.

Don't Teach on It if You're Struggling with It

We'll never be perfect, but any big or visible issues that are front and center in our lives right now aren't the issues about which we can offer effective leadership in our students' lives. If God is nudging us that we cannot teach or challenge adolescents on a certain topic because it's hindering our own spiritual journey, then we should allow someone else to take the lead.

Are We Doing What We Say to Do?

I discovered a simple truth about myself early on in youth ministry: I'll be the final victim of any messy game I conjure up and the poor, helpless target of any competition with a gotcha element involved. It took only one paintball war game and 20 paintball welts for me to learn this lesson the hard way. And although I vowed never to play paintball ever again (as I hid like a chicken behind a tree at Paintball Adventures outside of Tulsa), I did willingly put on the jumbo gloves for bouncy boxing once, and I got squashed in a sumo wrestling suit one Sunday morning as parents and students enjoyed the priceless entertainment of me waddling in a costume that made me as wide as I was tall.

You probably have a similar tale to tell. For us to try something crazy or lose our dignity in front of students is to win their admiration and earn a few minutes to really talk about life. So it's important that they see us as willing participants in our own harebrained youth ministry ideas. But it's also vital to our ministry effectiveness for us to heed the spiritual guidance we give to our students. We tell them to pray, but how much time do each of us spend in prayer? We encourage them to participate in worship and growth through a community of believers, but can we really count those weekly worship experiences as our time of renewal when we're distracted by our duties an hour later?

Even volunteer leaders can be so dedicated to their youth ministry role that they don't carve out any time to be in a small group or hang out with their spiritual peers. My friend Martha demonstrated this simple but essential truth to our leaders and students one Sunday. She rigged up an Igloo beverage cooler with a plastic cup securely taped under the spout. Sticking a little further out and secured under that first cup was another plastic cup. Martha pushed the button on the lever to fill the top cup. When it was more than full, it began to overflow into the cup beneath it. But not one drip of water went into the bottom cup until the first cup was completely full and then some. That's where kids need us to minister from—the "and then some." We don't have as much to give when we're giving from a deficit. But that's really a hard value to live. I've had to really practice what I've preached to students about tending their own spiritual journey.

MILE MARKER THIS...

Mile Marker Office

Make one room in your life a Mile Marker room that tells the story of your faith and purpose in pictures, artwork, furniture, and flow. Make it a museum of you that intrigues adolescents to ask for the story behind a crumpled picture or a scraped-up table. Gary and I have a friend who collected rare pieces of modern civilization to decorate his home office: A set of airplane seats, a discarded toilet, and many other strange collectibles! This room was quite a conversation starter, and it certainly allowed people to laugh and let down their guard for sharing their own story.

My Life Story

Every once in a while, retell your life story. Summarize it in a poem, relate it to a relevant song, or share the photographic highlights. Be sure to poke a little fun at yourself, share some lessons you learned, and give adolescents a chance to ask questions.

The "And Then Some" Factor

Rig up the Igloo beverage cooler as described in the previous paragraph, with one cup attached just beneath the spout. Give adults a cup and invite them to come up and drink from a cup filled with the water that overflows from the first filled cup. Lead a devotional time emphasizing what it means to pour into others' lives from the overflow in our own. Allow time for them to recognize their need as youth workers and parents to minister from the "and then some" factor in the lives of youth.

NO HALVES ABOUT IT

My senior English teacher transformed my life. She wasn't sweet or inspiring. Nor did I feel warm fuzzies from her when I entered her classroom. Quite frankly, at first I wondered if she even liked teaching high school students. I was also pretty sure she wasn't too impressed by me! She was brutally honest about my lack of skill and didn't hesitate to critique anyone's writing in front of the whole class. If someone's work was especially good or bad, she'd make copies of his or her essay for the entire class to pick apart and analyze. At the end of the group process, she'd pronounce the piece of writing "good" or "bad" with a colorful smattering of synonyms. Whenever she started passing out copies of students' work, everyone braced themselves for the coming onslaught. We never knew if our piece would turn out to be a style and approach to strive for or an example of what she never wanted to see again!

She was demanding. She didn't care about how much homework I had in my math class. That shouldn't stop me from reading the 50 pages she'd assigned or preparing for the unconquerable quiz she'd give the next morning. She wanted our work for her class to be top priority. She wanted all of my being engaged in what she was trying to teach me. Often, I resented her for wanting so much from me as a senior in high school. Didn't she know I had other hard classes, too? Didn't she know I was finishing my senior year at my third high school? Did she even care that I felt alone, depressed, and now, in her class, scrutinized?

But something in her fiery passion about writing and communicating appealed to me. There was no way I'd leave her class without showing her I could do what she challenged me to do. And I did. Even in college, I never had another English class that taught me as much as I learned as her student. She was, hands-down, the hardest teacher I've ever had. But because she was, here I am writing what she'd call a "run-on sentence" in a book, telling you stories, and giving you reasons why mile markers are important for students.

All of My Heart, Soul, and Strength

Like my senior English teacher, God wants all of me. He's asking me to respond to him with the very core and essence of my being. Some would say that God, who claims us as his own, is awfully demanding. Some might resent being asked to give God such unbridled devotion. But God knows what our investment of heart and soul cultivates down the road for us. God knows the wisdom, endurance, and peace that permeate our daily living when we love God with all that we are. God knows it will prepare us for the task of living out a life of authentic faith in front of others.

Sometimes I wonder about the distinction between giving all of my heart, all of my soul, and all of my strength. I see the direct correlation between my heart and soul, but strength seems to have a different thrust. Although the first two summarize all of who I am, the third summarizes all that I do. Even though it's used as a noun here, it actually seems to function as a verb in emphasis. For me, loving God with all of my strength is about the mental, physical, and spiritual efforts I exert to pursue God with all of my heart and soul, like exercising my faith enough to work up a sweat and build stamina.

When Weariness Sets In

I sat across the table from one of my leaders, listening to a confession of doubt and struggle. As one of my former students who'd been new to the church experience in early high school, he'd embraced following Christ with a fervent passion and gone on to be an exceptional leader with the middle school boys during his college studies. But on this day, he'd requested some time to talk about some stuff going on in his life. As he spoke, I heard the story of a person who couldn't reconcile the uncertainties of his soul with the realities of his life. His doubts had driven him to make some choices that he knew were risky, but he honestly shared that he wasn't quite ready to change directions. He was earnestly looking for answers in places like books on Eastern thought, and by visiting the local Buddhist temple a few times a month. He wanted to keep believing, but he also admitted he could no longer pretend to be sure of his faith in front of adolescent boys. So our conversation was about him reporting on his struggle as a believer and relinquishing his role as a leader.

No doubt he worried about my response. I was disappointed to hear where he'd been traveling on his faith journey, but I was also impressed that he unabashedly shared the condition of his heart. I'm so thankful that God prompted me not to give a 30-minute thesis in response to this young man's courageous confession! I accepted his resignation as a volunteer, but I tried to leave him with a few spiritual lifelines to cling to.

My basic encouragement to him that day was to keep praying no matter where his search took him. I urged him to look for God's fingerprint on anything that seemed good and right, even if he found it at the Buddhist temple. I also challenged him to live in the freedom that all truth is God's truth but not to forsake searching for that truth in the Bible. I assured him he'd find other books that revealed true things, but there was still only one Book that told God's Story in its entirety.

It takes effort and resolve to wrestle through the difficult questions of life, especially when the answers don't come quickly or don't come at all. And on the days when the only effort we can put forth is to honestly confess that we're weary of the struggle, God will provide strength for us. It's in these moments of thinking hard about unresolved issues in Scripture that I discover the deeper things of God. It's in holding on to faith and hoping in answers that I don't yet see that I'm able to press on.

> Students are watching how we live, how we make choices, and how we deal with pain. They need us to let down our guard and courageously face our own struggles. Otherwise, they won't have a spiritual mentor; they'll just have a tour guide.

MILE MARKER THIS...

Undivide Your Heart

Give students a chance to examine where their hearts might be divided between areas they've given to God and areas they're keeping hold of. Here are three object lesson ideas you can use:

- Simple and quick—You'll need paper hearts cut up like a jigsaw puzzle and pens for each student. Have students write down the important things and relationships in their lives on the puzzle pieces and then put together the puzzle while leaving out the pieces they haven't allowed God to have.
- Keepsake idea—You'll need wooden hearts (painted or stained) sawed into puzzle pieces. Students will use art pens or paints to do the same exercise. Then encourage them to take the heart home and put it on a dresser or nightstand where they'll see it. Then during personal prayer time or devotions, they can come back to the divided heart and evaluate the same areas of their lives when needed.
- Moderate prep—You'll need markers, river rocks, and a piece of cardboard or poster board cut into the shape of a heart for each student. Students should write the important areas of their lives on rocks and place the ones they've given to God inside the heart and the ones they still hold onto outside the heart.

Unpacking Church Baggage

Every so often, students need a chance to work through the misunder-standings, inconsistencies, and biases they'll most likely encounter at some point during their church experience. Whether they've heard something different from what we actually meant, observed leaders doing the op-posite of what they've proclaimed, or been exposed to a dogmatic and unwavering theology that's disconcerting, they need to debrief that kind of stuff so the shadows of doubt don't overwhelm the light of truth in their lives. Remember to—

- Clarify the truth in misunderstood messages
- Discuss the reality of our humanity, which means that even leaders miss the mark in big and small ways (including not doing what we say to do)

- Emphasize their right and responsibility to seek answers to questions, disagreements, and incongruities through Scripture, prayer, and wise counsel. Just because a leader says it, that doesn't make it true, right, or good.
- Always send them to Scripture to wrestle through these issues and then dialogue their responses together.

IF I'M IN, I'M ALL IN

There are things in our lives that we just can't be halfhearted about. Rappelling is one of those activities where a person has to fully commit. My first venture off the side of a rock was near Glendo Reservoir in Wyoming. To my 13-year-old eyes, it was a mammoth cliff with an upper bulge and then a steep vertical drop to the bottom. As I backed over the edge, I remember feeling some comfort that because of the bulge, my legs would not have to immediately go perpendicular to the rock in a typical sitting position. That assumption was wrong, however. I relied so much on staying in a standing position to maintain control that eventually my feet slipped off the edge of the bulge and left me dangling on the safety rope that was now parallel to the rock and about 60 feet above the ground. I received only a few scrapes from the fall, but I had a lot of fear about continuing on! I begged to be pulled back up, but the camp rappelling guide talked me through my dangling fears and eventually coached me down.

When I signed up to rappel at camp that week, I was captivated by the potential thrill of basically walking off a cliff. However, the reality that all of my body parts—even the ones that usually keep me standing on the ground—would have to commit to defying gravity was only fully present at the moment I took my first step backward. I'd have to let go and trust a new paradigm for normal human movement.

Following God is that same kind of adventure. If we're in, then we have to be all in. We have to engage our emotions and our brains. We have to not just say it but live it, too. That's not to say that we can achieve wholehearted commitment to God every second of every minute of every day. Daily life can be mundane, disappointing, overwhelming, stressful, uninspiring, or even agonizing. God understands that this journey isn't without obstacles and interruptions. God is a willing helper when life's strain tempts us to give up.

Hesitations

These are like spiritual potholes slowing our journey toward growth. It could be low self-confidence, a past failure, or lack of preparation, but usually there's a reason why we hesitate to be intentional about our own spiritual journeys. I might project other people's opinions of me onto how I believe God sees me.

For example, I'm not a detail-oriented person, and I'm often late. Therefore, many people in my life have categorized me as being disorganized because of those traits. The truth is, I'm a highly motivated, big-picture person who tries to fit more productivity into one minute than is humanly possible, which is why I tend to be tardy and miss the details. I've learned to take more time to purposefully gauge my clock commitments and surround myself with people who naturally see the details so my big-picture vision eventually becomes a completed project that gets finished on time. But for a long time in my life, I hesitated setting goals for personal growth and leadership if I thought people would respond with smirks and laughter about my big ideas taking shape. I didn't strive to read through the entire Bible or memorize Scripture because it seemed a foregone conclusion that I wouldn't finish well.

What I learned about myself was that I might not be the person who reads exactly one chapter in the Bible or 15 minutes every day, but I might spend one day in solitude, just exchanging prayer and listening time. The next day I might read my Bible for an hour and reflect on what I've read by writing in the margins. And the next, I might find my spiritual sustenance in a powerful movie or story. When I stopped allowing outside perspectives to highlight my personal deficits and instead began enjoying the way God wired me, I stopped hesitating to nurture my soul.

Distractions

Potholes are one type of irritation for travelers, and shoulder traffic is another. We've all been in that line of traffic that forms after there's an accident or incident along the shoulder or outer lane of the highway. Now sometimes we really do see a tragic scene when we finally pass by, but more often we get stuck in a long line of cars that's moving five miles an hour, only to discover that the incident along the side of the road was just a small fender bender with no apparent need to alter the flow of traffic (except for the distracted drivers who want to see what's going on).

These are the kinds of insignificant and sometimes life-altering scenarios that take our eyes off the road. We lose focus on the destination and put energy into something that isn't worth the time we allot it. Instead of receiving just a passing glance, it gets our full attention, and for enough time that we can no longer be wholehearted in the direction we were going. For me, I've had to learn when to turn off the voices of the world in my music, on my TV, and in what I read long enough to allow God to speak. That's hard for me to do because I don't do quiet well. I like background noise, singing along with my favorite songs, 24-hour news channels, and NPR segments. There will always be more to learn, more to do, and a line of requests for our time and energy. We have to be wise about when something has become a distraction.

Good Things That Aren't Great

I think this is the hardest part of the wholehearted commitment ideal, but arguably the most important. How often do we fill our lives with good things but not the best things? I believe God calls us to make a wholehearted commitment in our lives so we won't settle for second-best commitments. Every day I find opportunities to sacrifice the best choices for what seem to be very good choices. My physical fitness is vitally important to a healthy life, but it struck me one day that I spent a lot of energy not only exercising, but also fretting about my physical condition. To an observer, it probably didn't seem like a ridiculous amount of focus since I don't look like an Olympian. But when I recognized that the time I spent exercising my soul in prayer and study was only a fraction of my physical exercise time and that I didn't worry nearly as much about achieving higher goals in that area of my life, I decided I was allowing a good thing to be more important than the best thing.

MILE MARKER THIS...

Personal Inventory

Journal about the following questions and then come up with a plan to conquer hesitations and steer clear of distractions:

1. In what areas am I a hesitant person? How does it affect my faith and leadership?
2. What things about my personality or history might be helpful in understanding the hesitations that slow me down?
3. What gets me off track from my personal faith and purpose? How have distractions in my history impacted my life?
4. Why do I struggle with getting distracted by these things?

EXIT RAMP

I've always wanted to learn how to row. I watch women's rowing teams and feel utterly drawn to that sport. As I mentioned earlier, I'm not terribly coordinated, so although I've played some team sports, my athletic focus has become pursuits that don't require any human-to-human contact. Nevertheless, rowing still lingers in the back of my brain as something to try someday. Maybe I'm captivated by the pushing and pulling that helps the boat glide across the water, or maybe I'm just coveting the well-defined arms that come from the grueling workouts.

When I watched the Olympic rowing events on TV, I noticed that in a competition setting, a small army of coaches bike along the road next to the rowing channel. From that perspective, they're calling out directives to their team. The commentators even remarked that sometimes the coaches get so excited and caught up in their coaching that they forget to look ahead on their own path and may cause a bicycle wreck along the water.

More than anything, we should aspire to pass on a spiritual legacy to our students that we're living ourselves. We have to pay attention to where we're going and look ahead on our own spiritual journey before we can do much to lead them. If not, then someday they'll have to keep going ahead in their race while we untangle ourselves from a sideline collision.

1. What kind of spiritual journey have you been on lately? Are you tending your own soul before taking care of others? How?

2. Recall a story about someone who demonstrated wholehearted commitment in some pursuit or goal. What did you learn from that individual?

3. What can youth ministry do to encourage parents as journeyers and as spiritual leaders with their children?

4. What can parents do to support the ministry of a youth worker?

Stories from the Road

*"Repeat them again and
again to your children."*
Deuteronomy 6:7a (NLT)

CHAPTER

6

Every student trip I've ever led is chock-full of stories—usually the getting there and coming home stories. When I think about it, there are lots of bus detours on my résumé of trips. On the way to one particular skiing trip in Colorado, our bus driver took a wrong turn, in the middle of the night, and drove us halfway to Nebraska before he realized his mistake. At 3 A.M., I was mentally reciting, "Love is patient, love is kind…" as he told me that he didn't have an atlas because he never needs one!

A few years ago, our group got stuck (along with thousands of other spring break travelers) in Winter Park, Colorado, because of avalanches and treacherous roads created by the Hundred Year Storm. After being stranded for two extra days, we packed up the bus and headed for open road. Unfortunately, we made it only a quarter of a mile away from Young Life's Crooked Creek Ranch because the bus ran out of fuel on a hill leading out of the camp property. Later, the bus driver told me the bus's fuel gauge was broken, and he'd been estimating the fuel levels. His estimations bought us another night in the mountains.

There are pictures, videos, and even T-shirts that retell these stories. Whenever former students gather at our house for a reunion night, the conversations about how they're doing right now always start with the laughter and joyfulness of reminiscing about those stories. Rarely do they walk in the door and launch into a speech about all of their life-transforming experiences in our student ministry. Instead, they begin with the many "Remember when we…" stories, which lead to laughter and even more stories. And somewhere in between the tale about the junior guys throwing water balloons into the girls' second-story window at two in the morning and the story about how Ryan Myers' got second-degree burns on his legs from skiing in shorts on the last day—someone shares how she began to really trust God with her life on that trip.

God seems to be a big fan of stories, too. He didn't just hang a list of dos and don'ts from the sky and demand our cooperation with his will. Yes, Scripture is full of high expectations for intentional faith and living, but those commands are woven into a story that explains why God calls us to follow him and live a certain way. Although I found a few minor differences in the numbers, according to most of the Web sites containing Bible facts and trivia that I checked, there are 31,173 verses in the Bible. Of those verses, 6,468 of them are commands with specific instructions about life, relationships, worship, priorities, truth, and right versus wrong. The remaining 24,705 verses tell God's Story through the lives of the people who call him Lord and choose to walk the unique road of faith that God has paved for them.[8]

In the pages and biblical books surrounding these commands from God, there are narratives of those who put their hope in him and the life experiences of those who embraced God's commands and even struggled with them at times. These are the stories of determined, flawed, heroic, sacrificial, proud, wise, selfish, strong, and searching people—people like ourselves and the students we lead.

TELL THEM THE MOST IMPORTANT STORY

We all use stories to communicate truth and purpose. We illustrate stories, model stories, play stories, sing stories, and sneak stories into everyday life for our kids, over and over again. Stories teach. Stories encourage. Stories challenge. Stories motivate. But as youth workers, we can forget to tell the most important Story of all. How often do we meet people with a mental picture of God as a judge and spoilsport, but they don't know God's Story? They feel intimidated by God's demands, but they don't know about God's sacrifice? So many of our students claim to be Christians, but they cannot unpack what that identity means for them or the impact it has on their lives. These are the students who slip through our fingertips and miss out on the one Story they really need to hear! We must make sure that they hear, see, think, feel, and interact with God's Story. We must.

God's Story Is His Autobiography

No story is more powerful than the one God has written. It's a story in which God is both the Author and a participant. God's Story is an autobiographical account of his journey with humanity. It's the explanation of a world created by God's hand and the Divine imprint he pressed into our souls. It's God's account of humans losing their devotion and God not letting go because his goodness wouldn't allow him to forsake us.

In the first chapters of the Bible, he's God the Father—always with us, giving direction, demonstrating purpose, and igniting reverence deep within us. Then, in later chapters, an unexpected turn of events describes how God became God the Son, who walks with us while he's clothed in the same human skin that we wear. The earthly journey of Jesus the Son becomes the most painful and most beautiful turning point of God's Story. God's Son knowingly travels straight to his own demise. He walks right into a moment of giving up everything: Control, authority, respect, joy, understanding, devotion, love, and honor. God knows how his Story will unfold, and he writes it anyway. God doesn't hesitate. God doesn't second-guess himself. God just keeps writing.

The Bible's final chapters begin with the reversal of the doom, the redemption of what was lost. If Jesus had only lived and died, then it wouldn't be a story of the Divine but of mere humanity. But Christ lived, died, and lived again. By allowing his Son to lose every Divine inheritance and not interceding with a heavenly rescue, God demonstrates his unquantifiable love for his creation. By restoring life after a despairing loss, God demonstrates that he can breathe life into us—not once, but twice. First, to live and breathe in a world God created. And second, to live and breathe in the life God intended.

God's Story Is Ridiculous

One reason God's Story is the most important story we can tell is that it's ridiculous. We can't prove it happened. There isn't enough historical or archaeological evidence to unequivocally win a debate with someone requiring proof of this irrational existence and unlikely event in human history. But that's just the point. God doesn't offer his Story as a summary of absolutes, but rather as an invitation to experience his absolute goodness. God doesn't wish to impose concrete realities upon us. God wants to implant eyes of faith within us that recognize him as the one who saves.

In 1 Corinthians 1:18, Paul reminds the people of Corinth that the message of the cross is utter foolishness to those who look through a lens of human wisdom. For scientists, it remains an outlandish hypothesis that is impossible to test, thus giving no conclusions. Philosophers can trust only the human experience in the story. So they draw lessons and value from it, but they wouldn't dare trust in the unseen parts. Historians base their belief on the physical evidence left behind and the documented stories that still exist.

Students won't find a world that embraces God's Story; they'll find a world that tries to blot it out. They'll find resistance to it on a TV show like *The Secret Life of the American Teenager,* in which a student with a deep faith, Grace Bowman, is portrayed as being shallow and unsophisticated. They'll meet a friend who's suffered such a horrible tragedy that one can answer the question, "Why would God let this happen?" They'll encounter college professors who publicly chastise them for believing in something so naïve. Someday they might even get caught up in the daily drain of unfulfilling careers, struggling marriages, or financial and medical sand traps. Therefore, our students need to hear God's Story and all the hope, assurance, strength, and transformation it can infuse into their lives, because this ridiculous story is made possible only through the original Author.

God's Story Isn't Finished

I believe Jesus Christ is the one who saves me. I remember, at the tender age of seven, walking down the aisle during an evening worship service at First Southern Baptist Church in Casper, Wyoming, and responding to God's Story. It was compelling to me to grapple with the notion of such amazing love and sacrifice. As a little girl, I understood the part of the story that any grade school student would understand. But now I understand that Christ was at work with his Father in the first moments of creation, writing a story of redemption for all people. I also understand that the Story is still being written. The revelation of the Story has been completed, but the telling of it is still being narrated in our lives. I now know that I'm saved, but God has been at work saving me—and others throughout history—for a long time, and there will be a day when we experience that salvation fully.

When students experience God's Story as one that's still happening to them and for them, they want to hear more. When Jesus' role in history becomes more than just a remarkable life to emulate, when students hear the message of the cross and their human and eternal destinies suddenly collide, when they see their purpose in God's purpose—that's when another chapter in God's Story is written, because more people have discovered their part in it.

MILE MARKER THIS...

Picture Threads

Tell the Story of God through different picture threads in Scripture. Share it while reflecting on the idea of a covenant from Genesis to Revelation. Explain it through the lens of sacrifice, from Abraham's close call with Isaac to all that Jesus lost on the cross and the cost his disciples were willing to pay to follow him. Illustrate it with the idea of kingdom and show all the places in Scripture where a kingdom is in the forefront of a story, just as living in God's kingdom is something we should strive for. And there are so many others: The "I ams" in John, all those who qualify as the "least of these" in Luke, and the parables scattered throughout the Gospels, for example.

HELPING STUDENTS SEE GOD IN OUR STORIES

Your Story

I remember the night I had a girls' sleepover at my house. Gary was away on business, and we didn't have any children yet. I extended an invitation to the girls in our youth group and a few adult leaders to come over for movies, popcorn, chocolate, and lots of late-night talk. At midnight one girl worked up the courage to ask me some pretty personal questions about my dating relationships in high school and beyond. In telling her the story of my own faith journey and the regrets and lessons I'd experienced along the way, she heard that God was real and true in the midst of my life's struggles.

The good and the bad from our own stories can play a redemptive part in our students' lives. Both are needed to connect with students who, like us, have good and bad stuff going on at the same time. I always tell students that because I was always "the strong Christian girl" in my youth group, no one ever questioned whether or not I was able to maintain that strength in a dating relationship. I had a lot of good things happening in my life, but I also felt helpless to get some things right during my adolescence.

Our students will be inspired to make a higher commitment and wiser choices when we encourage them that we trusted God and did the right thing at a pivotal crossroads. With so many voices dooming them to an adolescent journey fraught with bad choices, they need to hear someone say, "I know it's possible because I did it." They'll also find comfort and release in the knowledge that people they admire can miss the mark, too. Scripture doesn't sugarcoat the mistakes of its greatest spiritual heroes, so we shouldn't hide our shortcomings either.

> God doesn't offer his Story as a summary of absolutes, but rather as an invitation to experience his absolute goodness. God doesn't wish to impose concrete realities upon us. God wants to implant eyes of faith within us that recognize him as the one who saves.

The Parents' Stories

I wrote earlier about asking my male leaders to plan a guys' rite of passage event a few years ago. (See chapter 3.) As a ministry team, we were inspired to create this event from the experiences of youth workers we heard speak at Youth Specialties' National Youth Workers Convention. From the beginning, dads were given a leading role in taking their sons through the experience. Each father walked a literal path with his son around a small lake, where together they encountered different men who talked to the boys about what being a man after God's own heart really means (Acts 13:21-22). But before the boys heard from these men, they heard from their own fathers. Maybe for the first time, these boys' dads shared with them about their own faith journeys.

One of the most beautiful gifts we can give to parents is the opportunity to tell their children their own stories of following God. As a parent, I know I can get wrapped up in the laundry list of household and academic to-dos and forget to share spiritual exchanges with my children. When we create a venue for parents to step out of their daily busyness and become a voice of spiritual purpose, their children are better able to understand their own spiritual journeys. As children, we often see ourselves in our parents' story.

When we encourage conversations about life and faith beyond an event planned for parents and children, we help them gain a deeper understanding of each other that may have gotten lost in all of the daily tussles of the average adolescent-parent conflict. It's true for any human relationship, really—when we allow God to participate in our journeys with one another, it's impossible not to catch a glimpse of what God sees in us. Thus, we dig deeper to understand each other, we're more intentional to demonstrate our love for the other person, and we begin to trade in our earthly and unimportant expectations of each other for eternal, enduring ones.

I realize we cannot achieve this with every family; but I believe that as youth workers, we truly fulfill the heart and purpose of Deuteronomy 6:4-9 every time we help a parent pass on a faith legacy and be a force of spiritual strength in their children's lives. We help make it possible for parents and their teenagers to share in the joy of following God together.

The Stories of Friends and Strangers

One group of high school guys had been very active in our student ministry since early middle school. But once they reached ninth grade, I struggled to find a male leader who could connect with them. They were confident, close friends with an abundance of talent and personality between them. But leaders who could challenge them to the next level hadn't emerged.

One day I was skimming a list of the names of adults in our church, while hoping God would miraculously highlight a name in "heavenly yellow," when the name of an attorney jumped out at me. I knew his daughters when they were in high school, and I considered them to be tremendous young women who lived out their faith. I figured that said something positive about the people who parented them, so I called and asked him to lead this group of guys. I can't remember if he gave me an answer that day. But when he did respond, his only condition was, "as long as I don't have to talk about sex!" Of course, I promised him that topic would come up and he'd find the words when it did.

Within months, the guys nicknamed him "Coach." They loved that he refereed rugby, was a smart and accomplished attorney, and really enjoyed giving me a hard time. He had much to teach them through his own story, which included a life spent following Christ but also enduring a difficult divorce. Teaching from his perspective also meant requiring his guys to teach each other. He saw their spiritual depth and required them to prepare lessons and be "as iron sharpens iron" in each other's lives (Proverbs 27:17).

One Sunday morning while I was getting ready for our high school gathering, I asked that group of guys (now juniors) to help move some of the furniture. They informed me that they took instructions only from Coach. I quickly sensed their humor and unity in harassing the youth minister, so I looked at Coach and asked him to please tell his guys to move the stinking furniture.

Early on I knew I wouldn't be the spiritual force in these guys' lives. For one, I believe my gender limited my ability to influence and disciple them. Two, they just needed a different personality and camaraderie from what was natural for me. They knew I cared about them, but I knew I didn't inspire them. So I found someone whose life experiences and style would resonate in their lives.

We should constantly be in prayer and on the lookout for unique adults who may not know they can guide adolescents on a journey of faith and purpose. We should be on alert to discover authors, speakers, community leaders, and cultural icons whose stories can also make inroads into the adolescent experience.

I'm encouraged by the words of Hebrews 12:1—

> Therefore, since we are surrounded by such a great cloud of witnesses, let us throw off everything that hinders and the sin that so easily entangles. And let us run with perseverance the race marked out for us.

We don't enter into this journey alone; God has surrounded us with a huge "cloud of witnesses" who are cheering us on in our faith and spurring us on to run our race of faith with all of our might. Students need to surround themselves with a crowd of witnesses, too.

They may hear us speak or watch us lead, but that doesn't mean we need to be the only voice that speaks into their lives. They need to hear the stories of friends—people they can look to for guidance and help. They need to hear the stories of strangers also—heroes in Scripture and trailblazers in history—and people in their immediate world who speak boldly about following Christ and live out that faith courageously.

MILE MARKER THIS...

Story Gifts

Oftentimes when adolescents are asked about their parents' faith story, they don't know it. Somehow that very important narrative doesn't get told in families, so parents who aren't quite sure how to verbalize their own stories at first may wish to write it in a letter and give it to their kids as a gift. Maybe it becomes a memorable stocking stuffer or is given during a rite-of-passage event. Maybe Dad saves it for the day when his son or daughter is in trouble and really needs to hear his story about God's redemption in his life. It most likely will become a treasured spiritual keepsake that keeps illuminating the road ahead.

Mentors to Us, Strangers to Them

Ask someone who was a significant spiritual mentor in your life to share his story with a group of teens. They'll experience a glimpse of spiritual legacy, hear the story as you did when it impacted your life, and hopefully show them what they can experience with an adult who walks alongside their lives.

The Family that Prays Together and for Each Other

Give parents and students the tools and encouragement to share prayer needs with each other and spend some time doing prayer exercises together. Make a homegrown prayer guide with Scriptures and ancient prayer rituals that will help them to get started. Encourage them to take turns leading, as family members feel comfortable. The purpose of this exercise is to facilitate a God-view of each other. When we pray for someone else, we can't help but see what God sees in that person. We also have a better understanding of an individual's story when we experience someone's conversations with God.

TELL THEM AGAIN

Picture yourself standing with a group of parents and church leaders when one of your favorite students says, "Tell them about the time you dropped the f-bomb!" Then picture your ministry career evaporating before your eyes. Okay, well, I didn't lose my job, but I did accidentally use that expletive in front of my student leaders one warm Wednesday afternoon. It was an unintentional gaffe resulting from my brain moving faster than my mouth, and the word that my tongue and lips produced was not the word my brain was thinking. Now, in the interest of full disclosure, I've cussed during my lifetime. However, I don't like that particular curse word, and I'd never use it on purpose!

Not surprisingly, my students love that story! They love remembering how everyone literally fell on the floor laughing after several seconds of pure shock and silence. They love telling people that I do, in fact, have a potty mouth and they have proof. But really, I believe they love reliving that moment of hilarity and are encouraged by the humility I had to demonstrate in such a blunder. It's one story among many that's retold because we share it and it says something—actually, a lot—about the honesty and joy in our relationships.

Repetition Helps Them Remember

If students can recall that 30-second vignette over and over again, imagine what they'll remember from our lessons and conversations if God's Story is always before them. I remember sometimes dismissing a well-known passage in Scripture for a different lesson choice because I thought our students had heard it a lot. What I should have done in those instances was ask myself if my students needed to hear the story again with a fresh voice, a different perspective, or a creative medium.

> When students experience God's Story as one that's still happening to them and for them, they want to hear more.

Retelling Strengthens the Message

Every year, a local church offers a sermon series focused around the movies. So each Sunday for four weeks, in between the movie segments, they take excerpts from popular films and weave a biblical message about life and knowing God. One week, I came away with an overwhelming truth to hold on to from Psalm 39:4 (NLT): "LORD, remind me how brief my time on earth will be. Remind me that my days are numbered—how fleeting my life is." I got it. I don't have any time to waste. That truth is imprinted on my brain because not only did the pastor say it multiple times during the message, but also the verse quietly faded onto the screen in between the movie clips and the pastor's speaking.

Now, the story from that week's movie didn't just entertain me and give me warm fuzzies. It also reminded me to make the most of my life and earnestly follow after God. It's not the first time I've contemplated that truth. But hearing the story of human finiteness and God's infiniteness through a character in a movie and seeing those words again and again certainly made the truth more real to me. If we can help students see the Story of God as relevant and true to the moment they're in, then we'll help them enter into that Story, make it their own, and write it upon their own hearts.

MILE MARKER THIS...

Service of Repetition

Plan a service where the same passage is repeated over and over again through different mediums. For example, have someone read it and ask an artist to paint or chalk its main idea on a blank canvas while students worship with songs that use its theme. Invite a testimony that illustrates the meaning of the Scripture and ask students to write a prayer for themselves that uses the words of the passage that are especially powerful for them. Repeat the Scripture in any way that deepens the imprint it leaves on students' hearts.

Interview a Stranger

Take a group of adolescents into a gathering of youth workers and believers they don't know and have them interview one or more people about their own journeys. Give them a list of questions to get them started. Hopefully they'll find the stories so interesting that the conversations will flow with ease. Later, let them share the highlights with each other and tell how the experience impacted them.

God's Story in Real Life

I've heard how youth workers have given their students an opportunity to share where they saw God show up in their lives during the past week. Some people call them "God sightings." This exercise is a little more specific in that youth are given a Scripture story or passage to use as they contemplate how God might demonstrate it in their lives during the coming week. When they return in seven days, have them share vignettes and journal entries describing how they noticed God's truth in that Scripture making an appearance in their lives over the previous days.

Don't Get Lost in One Translation

This one is simple. Keep the truth of God's Story rich and fresh by using more than one translation of a Scripture passage. Different words and phrases in various translations connect with students in a way that your favorite translation may not. This is one of the easiest ways to help Scripture come alive for kids.

Retell a Story Without Words

This is another silent lesson, but this time the teachers are objects and actions—with no words. Present a drama without dialogue, such as an adaptation of *Ragman* by Walter Wangerin Jr., so as to use only gestures to communicate how the Ragman is offering new rags for old and the way that transforms those who give up their old rags for new ones.[9] Footwashing services can easily be done without talking, and parables are full of vivid details that would be simple to illustrate with only props and actions.

EXIT RAMP

This past summer my son walked into a marvelous church foyer encompassed with high ceilings and a rotunda of gothic arches. It was breathtaking. It was also resounding. Garrison quickly figured out that if he yelled—or whispered, for that matter—he'd hear his own echo bouncing all around the room. He loved that sense of being surrounded by his own voice, so he just kept bellowing into it.

The Story of God and his walk with us is the original Voice calling us to step into a life and journey with him. His narrative is written through the lives of ancient people and published through the retelling of each generation's unique story that's still connected to those who first believed. There is an echo of echoes throughout history where people find their humanity intersecting with God's Divinity. Our job is to let students hear the refrain of that extraordinary Story so it can echo into their lives over and over again.

1. When have you felt a connection with your spiritual ancestry? How would you like to offer that same connection to the adolescents in your life?

2. What's a part of your story that would teach, encourage, or inspire an adolescent?

3. Who is someone you know that students should meet and hear his story?

4. List one or two ways that you could offer a fresh telling of God's Story to students.

Conversations on the Road

"Talk about them when you are at home and when you are on the road, when you are going to bed and when you are getting up."
Deuteronomy 6:7b (NLT)

CHAPTER

7

My favorite acronym from my ministry years at Redeemer Covenant is D.I.G. It stands for "Deeper Into God," but I really loved the name because of the artwork we used with it. A coworker brought me a hilarious picture of a pug-like dog digging in the dirt for a bone. But what made the image so funny was that the vantage point was from behind the dog's back end.

After I created great covers for our student notebooks using the image of that dog digging in the dirt, I put together a fairly predictable study format of fill-in-the-blank outlines. Even now as I look back on those studies, I believe the material was strong and the handful of students who attended the study got something good out of it. However, the title implied that students would be getting dirty and doing something offbeat, not sitting and listening to an adult who enjoys the sound of her own voice.

What I realized is that I don't always have to have a separate program for students to dig deeper into God's Story. Every gathering—whether it be fun or serious, for an individual or multitudes of students—has the potential for those "Ah-ha!" and "So what?" experiences (which we talked about in chapter 3) without it having to be a "sit down, be quiet, and listen" teaching environment. Teachable moments don't require me to talk every time. Shared truths don't always have to be delivered in outline form.

The beauty of the instructions in Deuteronomy 6:7 is that we're encouraged to talk about the important matters of faith wherever we are and whatever we're doing. So in an attempt to redeem my favorite acronym, I've revamped the name and added what I learned from my first attempts at helping students dig deeper in all kinds of different places in their lives.

DEEPER INTO GOD'S STORY (D.I.G.S.)

In 1987, smack-dab in the middle of my sophomore year, I moved from Casper, Wyoming, to Aurora, Colorado. Transferring schools had its share of academic and social hurdles, but one teacher made all the difference for me—Ken Carmann. As a former defensive tackle for the University of Nebraska at Kearney and an eleventh round pick in the 1967 NFL draft (chosen by the San Francisco 49ers[10]), Mr. Carmann was a massive man who took up the entire doorframe of his classroom.

I quickly realized two things. First, Mr. Carmann's classroom was a shrine to geometry. He oozed with passion for the topic, rigging up three-dimensional problems that took days for his students to solve. They'd visit his classroom before and after school to study the problem some more, hoping he'd give them a hint at the answer.

Second, he really cared about his students in ways that transcended his teaching. Being a jock, he liked to call us by our last names. He even called me "Wyoming" a few times, just to highlight that he remembered my story of having just moved to a new city and school. His class was always in session because of his open-door invitation for student-teacher interaction. And even when there weren't any challenge assignments built in the middle of his classroom, students were always dropping by.

Surprisingly, there was never a dull moment during geometry. Mr. Carmann wanted his students to do more than just learn geometry; he wanted us to discover all the places where it shows up in our daily lives. He didn't just stand at the front of the classroom and instruct; he led his students on a geometric adventure. Our class was about more than just paper and pencils and answers; it was about possibilities and discussions and applications.

I don't know what Mr. Carmann believed spiritually. But I do know he had a natural gift for walking students down a path that roused our intellect and deepened our understanding of what previously seemed to be a mundane subject. He did it by never being satisfied with one way of teaching us. If one problem didn't get our attention, then he'd try another. If something didn't make sense, then he'd illustrate the problem another way. In addition to teaching basic principles, he asked lots of questions (and intently listened to ours), debated our conclusions, fielded our confusions, and never tired of dialoguing with us about math and life. That might be why his teaching was so influential in students' lives. For him, it wasn't just about the good math information we'd learn in his class. It was about the lives we were living and how math was a part of them.

Sometimes in ministry we unintentionally make spiritual maturity about information—memorizing Scripture, reciting tenets of our church doctrine, learning about timelines in church history, reading the Bible from cover to cover, or even just creating that "sit down, be serious, and listen" atmosphere that students experience quite often in their lives already.

If Ken Carmann could make such a powerful impact on students during the same hour each day and in one classroom space with nothing but desks, chalkboards, and a problem rigged with a tripod and tape, think of the universe of potential we have in youth ministry to walk and talk creatively with our students in all kinds of places and at all different times in their week! All of those good things we want to teach them about knowing and following God aren't much of a force in their lives if they never journey where they'll encounter the power of Scripture, learn to think for themselves theologically, or walk in the footsteps of someone else's historical or biblical faith journey.

I believe Scripture tells us to keep talking to our spiritual and biological children about our relationship with God not only because it helps them learn and remember, but also because those literal and symbolic conversations on the road of faith move them to a deeper place of spiritual maturity—a real place of identity that intersects with a real confidence in knowing a God who knows them. Students need us to push them to reach farther and work harder to understand who they are in the light of a good and great God.

But to borrow Jim Rayburn's famous words, "It's a sin to bore a kid with the Gospel of Jesus Christ."[11] We shouldn't leave them feeling overwhelmed and intimidated by the information about their spiritual journey without staying alongside them to dialogue, examine truth, grapple with contradiction, toil over complexities, and squirm about our own inconsistencies. Hopefully, doing so will leave our students as wiser and more mature people who've logged many accumulated miles while figuring out who they are and what they believe.

Let's take students on a fast-paced exploration to unearth sacred truths upon which to live and build their lives. Let's help them go deep and get dirty with the messiness of that which is the legacy of Christ followers. Here are some launching points for leading students into spiritual D.I.G.S.

DIG DEEPER

Where Are They?

The most effective start I ever had to a small-group season was when I asked each house group leader to assess their group's spiritual, emotional, and social profile. It seemed vitally important to let the adults who knew the students best tell me what their needs and challenges would be in the coming months. A handful of the groups had already been together at least one year, so their leaders could look back at group dynamics and previous studies and gatherings to determine where they were on their adolescent pilgrimage. They could also ask their group members—all together or individually—for an update on the external and internal issues they were facing each day.

For new groups, leaders couldn't just plunge into the deep end of sharing and learning before they'd had some time to build a foundation of friendship and trust for their small group adventure. So we encouraged these leaders to have their groups spend a few weeks eating together, sharing their own stories, and learning as much about each student's life as possible. We encouraged them to observe how students interacted with one another and what growth possibilities and roadblocks these connections might produce. Whether a group consisted of students who were brand-new to each other or old friends, once we began asking, "Where are they on their adolescent journey?" we quickly became more effective at figuring out where they needed to go.

Where Do They Need to Go?

After we've figured out a student's general location on his or her path to maturity, it's important to set some goals regarding how far we can take him or her in the pursuit of a sometimes-elusive purpose and identity. When we looked at our small groups that year, we saw a genuine picture of runners training for a spiritual marathon. One or two groups were at the very beginning—no training or even insight into what following Christ looks like. Others had been in training and were more adept at the long distances, but they were certainly encountering obstacles and pain along the way. And then there were a few whose training depth and mileage increases made it vital to keep them focused, challenged, and inspired to keep going.

Within each group was a wide array of student experiences that may or may not have fit the general group description. That's why I found it so beneficial to release my leaders to know their students' needs better than I did. I might "know" student culture in general, but they "knew" their students' lives and immediate circumstances. I tried to break up one group of 20 girls more than once because I was convinced they wouldn't be able to maintain such a large number throughout high school. They proved me wrong.

During their second-to-last year in the group, I strongly encouraged—even warned—them that I'd eventually split them up once some of them got to know the new leaders I added. But the lead leader told me the girls didn't want to separate, and she wanted to honor their request. She had a plan to push their spiritual development and give them more accountability in their faith. So I let go of that endeavor early in their junior year. Just last spring, I stopped by one of their final house-group gatherings and hugged more than 20 girls (now seniors)! In most of their stories, I sensed more self-assurance, less self-scrutiny, fewer exterior veneers, and more inward reflection. In short, maturity!

Usually intimate group dynamics weaken with more than eight to ten people, but these girls were the exception—not only did they maintain their group, but they also sustained each other. In this case, their leader wisely discerned and listened to them about where their group needed to go. She saw their request as an opportunity to stretch them in true Christian community. If we know where students are but don't attempt to stretch them and take them somewhere deeper in their personal understanding, we'll be causing them to spin their wheels instead of helping them take flight.

What Will Help Get Them There?

We had a basic curriculum outline for each grade and gender, but it was purely a guide. After several years of short-circuiting the effectiveness of our small group ministry with sameness, we decided to try to match our study or curricula to fit each group's personality and needs. We wanted to help them move beyond where they were in their personal growth and get to where we hoped they could go. That year the high school ministry staff met with each small-group leader to talk about where their group was and where they needed to go and to offer guidance as to what might help them get there. We brought in several books and curricula as suggested possibilities, but when those didn't fit a group's profile, we went on a mission with the group leaders to find or develop something that would work best for their groups.

We also spent time evaluating how the group's meeting time needed to be organized. Did they need half of the allotted time to just hang out and relax in a safe and encouraging place? Were they more like Old Faithful—gushing with another spiritual inquiry that set discussion in motion for two hours every week? Would the topics we hoped to discuss with eighth grade boys be best taught with lots of movement and activity? Would they have a richer experience if instead of us giving them something, we required them to give something away?

One of the mottos we frequently applied was "Girls Talk, Boys Walk." Naturally, it wasn't true in every case; but most of the time, girls could sit in a circle to listen and share for much longer than the guys could, especially in the middle school and early high school years. So if a male leader was frustrated with his guys' lack of introspection, we encouraged him to play basketball for an hour and sit and talk for 15 to 30 minutes afterward. Or he could weave a conversation into a round of Frisbee golf and wrap it up over burgers at Carl's Jr.'s.

Discussing the important organizational and environmental questions with our volunteers helped us fine-tune our ministry and give students a deeper and more challenging experience. I believe this also helped our students see the gospel as being more meaningful in their world.

We also made sure to ask our leaders about their personal leadership styles and preferences. Some loved creating their own lessons and group experiences. Those kinds of leaders sometimes scare youth ministers because we can't read them from cover to cover like we can a published curriculum. We must be careful not to stifle the passion and giftedness of a leader just because he or she might have a different and creative way of getting students to the same destination we're aiming for.

Every once in a while, a leader wanted to teach something I disagreed with. That's when the timeless truth of "major on the majors and minor on the minors" is a youth minister's wisest defense. If a leader's personal perspective didn't have any general foundation in Scripture, I'd certainly intervene before I let him or her present his or her bias to students. If my theological or stylistic difference with them wasn't crucial to the central message of the gospel and was reasonably supported by Scripture, then I'd try to let go of my bias, believing it would only enrich students' spiritual growth to see healthy dialogue and debate in the church. It certainly takes a little more time and gentle oversight to know where a leader is going with a lesson, but we'll see a greater movement of God in students' lives if we release more leaders to really lead.

Other leaders want to use a book or a guide or a plan that someone else created. That's great, too. There's plenty of good stuff out there that will strengthen their ministry to students and free them up to really focus on relationships.

And we can't forget those leaders who can't sit still. Guess which students we give to them? You've got it—the students who can't sit still, either! In these leaders, students will find someone who understands how they tick, and the result will be adolescents who thrive because their small group may be one of the only places where their energy levels aren't considered a deficit or flaw.

The Students We Can Lose

No matter how well your ministry is structured, it likely won't meet every student's needs. And we don't want these teens to lose heart on their spiritual journey just because our ministry format isn't a good fit for them.

One such student comes to mind. He began attending my youth group at Redeemer when he was in middle school. When I met him just before his ninth grade year, it seemed like a cloud of uncertainty was troubling his soul. He was always gracious and sincere, but I sensed doubt in his eyes. To add to the ambiguities in his life, I couldn't find a small-group leader for him and the other guys in his grade. I worried about the stuff he was wrestling with deep inside because I had a pretty good guess about his struggles. Many times during his freshman year, I'd pray and ask God to please send the right people to guide him through this difficult leg of his journey.

A series of God-inspired circumstances began to unfold in answer to my prayers. First, he took a job at the church, and the staff took a personal interest in his life. On Sunday mornings he heard about a God who loved him no matter what, and then every day after school he experienced church leaders who nurtured his life no matter what. I believe he began to see that he wasn't just hanging bulletin board signs or moving furniture, but he was participating in something far greater. I continued to pray for him to feel the unseen dimension of God's grace and power at work in people's lives, including his own.

It wasn't long before we discovered other avenues to share life with him. He was a talented drummer, so we sought him out to play percussion and invited his band to play for events. He was great with little kids, so his job as a one-man set-up crew for the children's ministry sometimes stretched into a more relational role. Redeemer also became a safe place for him to acknowledge his doubts on the road of faith. Some of those early hallway conversations with pastors became mentoring relationships that allowed him to process the struggles in his life.

I briefly chatted with him before he left for college. As we talked I searched, but couldn't find that fog of confusion in his countenance anymore. I saw a brightness and clarity that hadn't been visible four years earlier. I knew he didn't move from a place of many struggles to none. But I also knew that even without a typical student small-group experience, people kept talking to him about life and faith in all kinds of places.

From what he told me and the reports I received about him sharing his story with Redeemer students about a month before graduation, I felt a deep well of gratitude rise up in my soul, knowing that in the midst of the many storms he'd weathered on the adolescent road, godly people—including his parents—had stepped onto that road with him time and again. They talked and walked him through scary stuff. And then they kept talking to him, and they didn't give up. I wholeheartedly believe those conversations will always anchor his spiritual journey.

MILE MARKER THIS...

Roundtable of Burning Questions

Gather a group of students in a circle around a round table. Have several large candles lit on the table. If you can pull off this gathering outside, use a small bonfire and put a round table near it—but not too close! Make sure your students know ahead of time that this is the "Round Table of Burning Questions" and they can write down any burning question they may have about God, life, or faith. Students can place their questions either on the table or in a basket that gets passed around the circle and then dumped onto the table (but hopefully not on the burning candles).

Have a team of wise and discerning adults who've modeled a life of personal study and vibrant faith on hand to serve as an impromptu panel. One youth worker should be the host and introduce any unknown adults ahead of time. Be sure to highlight the reasons you asked these adults to participate—let students know why you admire them and their spiritual insights. Then go through the questions one at a time, offering students Scripture passages that address their questions and insights from the panel. Offer students a journal note sheet that they can use to take notes and come back to later.

Youth Ministry at Large

Invite parents and youth leaders to brainstorm how to reach any teenagers "at large" in your church. These are students who aren't yet involved in the existing youth ministry programs. You may be able to go through a list of known at-large students and find adults who are willing to pursue mentoring relationships with them. There may also be two or three leaders who have a heart for these students and will provide leadership to a ministry plan to reach at-large students through common interests. It can take lots of different shapes, but it's most important that the conversation gets started.

DIG INTO

Once we have a sense of where our students are on their journeys, where they need to go, and how we'd like to guide them to that new place of maturity, we should brainstorm some ideas for how we can help them experience the Story of God, instead of just knowing it.

In 2 Peter 1:16, Peter writes, "For we did not follow cleverly devised stories when we told you about the coming of our Lord Jesus Christ in power, but we were eyewitnesses of his majesty." Peter is reminding the believers that this story, which is being repeated all around the Roman world, isn't a fable. It's true, and Peter had a front row seat to the events that are described.

Enter the Act

Obviously, we can't give students the same unique experience that the first disciples had. But the Story is no less personal or powerful in their lives today. The author of Hebrews cannot say enough about God's Story being a phenomenon in the lives of those who receive it:

> For the word of God is alive and active. Sharper than any double-edged sword, it penetrates even to dividing soul and spirit, joints and marrow; it judges the thoughts and attitudes of the heart. Nothing in all creation is hidden from God's sight. Everything is uncovered and laid bare before the eyes of him to whom we must give account. (Hebrews 4:12-13)

This is the description of a Story that penetrates people's lives and leaves them visibly changed. It's a Story that goes to the core of who we are—humans with the breath of God within us. This is the Story that students must enter into.

We need to help our students have a genuine experience of God's Story. They must feel the heat from the furnace as they hear the death sentence pronounced upon three young Israelite men being held captive in Babylon who wouldn't surrender their belief in God—even if it cost them their lives (Daniel 1–3). They must walk along a deserted road, listening in on Jesus' conversation with two grieving believers on their way to Emmaus. At first they didn't recognize Jesus as being the one they'd just lost. But when they finally realized who this man was, they understood that the One they'd dared to believe in had been walking with them all along (Luke 24:13-35).

When students enter into the act of Communion, we want them to practice the promise that's threaded throughout the Old and New Testaments: God is in the business of buying us back from the debt of our sin and the sins of others. This promise echoes in the Passover meal and again during Jesus' last Seder with his disciples. Adolescents need to hear the voices from the past, smell the incense given at Jesus' birth and death, feel the grit of sand between their toes from walking miles to get a glimpse of the God who loves them and calls them into a life with him.

The Bread That Gives Life

My mother has taught me many things, but one of the best lessons I've learned from her is how to make bread. Our family specialty is cinnamon rolls; but really, we love bread of any kind. Kneading is a very important part of bread making. I've tried skipping that step once or twice, and the dough never rises properly. Kneading is important because mixing the flour and moisture (usually water) creates a necessary gluten web that expands and traps the carbon dioxide as it's released from the mixing of yeast and flour. That expanding web is what makes the bread rise. So the more the dough is kneaded and worked, the more that flour and moisture can find each other and add on to the gluten web as it expands.

Students need us to knead them as well. They need us to impart truth to them and inspire them to embrace a life of following God. They also need dialogue that puts that information and inspiration to the test. They need scenarios in which they must decide where to find truth and how to apply it. They'll thrive when they walk in an environment in which one complexity links to another question that helps them realize an answer with eternal significance.

My passion is to give adolescents a taste of sustenance that will continue to expand and grow throughout their lives. We have to not only mix all of the ingredients of faith and purpose, but also keep working through the story, going back, talking more, debating some, back and forth, pressing, stretching, and shaping through our conversations and teaching so their faith will grow and a belief that sustains their lives will rise from the kneading we cause them to endure.

Question Marks and Exclamations

The beauty of conversation is that unlike traditional teaching, it's an exchange. I offer you a thought; you respond with a question. After we banter back and forth several times, one of us caps off the dialogue with a conclusion or yet another question. It may be hilarious or gut-wrenching. It could contain anger or excitement. It might actually be rather ordinary but still refreshing. Conversations with our students before, after, or during our more formal teaching moments will give breadth and dimension to the shaping of their identities, especially if we allow room for question marks and exclamations to be expressed.

There are three kinds of questions that are important for students to ask. And we must create safe spaces in which they can ask them.

The first one is the dangerous question. It's the kind that many students see as a make-or-break inquiry. If they ask if they might be gay, will they forever be rejected? If they admit they're skeptical of this whole God thing, will anyone meet them in their disbelief? If they judge the church against their political ideology and voice their opinions, will they be alienated? These are the dangerous questions that require students to feel safe before they ask. And we must be courageous enough to wade into them with students, even when clarity and certainty are difficult to pin down.

The second is the indefinite answer question. Teenagers are great at posing questions for which there are no easy answers. Some of their questions could be addressed by a lengthy scriptural study and thoughtful commentary, but there are certainly topics in our faith that we can tackle and still not find an emphatic answer.

My daughter just realized a few weeks ago that there's no mention of dinosaurs in the Bible. She wanted to know why and if that should change what she believes about prehistoric times or creation. My husband and I affirmed her question and dove into an elementary version of embracing science and Scripture. But we still couldn't give her a simple answer as to why there's no mention of dinosaurs in the Bible.

When it's appropriate, we should encourage students to see what conclusions they can draw from a personal study pursuit. It's also okay to eventually offer honest insights about the things we can't explain and continue to search and dialogue together. That conversation is a great segue into the topic of how "faith is being sure of what we hope for and certain of what we do not see" (Hebrews 11:1).

The third question is the one we ask and don't answer (at least at first). It's so good to send students home while they're still wondering. There are mysterious things of God that aren't mysteries. There are wonderful explanations about life that aren't obvious—but they aren't secrets either. If we always ask a question and then answer it before students have time to get uncomfortable with it, then they'll still get the answer but will miss out on the mystery and the wonder.

As long as we don't send our students away in fear or create an atmosphere of competition, and as long as we offer them some helps and tools for their search, then leaving teenagers with a question to wrestle with now and then is a healthy part of their maturation. Our conversations with students need to have some "I got it!" moments, too. When they have the opportunity to express some things that have come together for them or share a new understanding or experience, it reinforces the lessons they're learning. It also impacts their small-group peers.

Young Life does this so well on the last night of their camps. This part of the camp experience is called "Say So," and students are asked to share if God has made a difference in their life that week. It's so powerful to watch how their own courage to stand and tell the story that God is writing in their lives strengthens them right there in the moment. And the answers they've found mean even more to them after they've shared them with someone else. It's equally powerful to watch their words penetrate their friends' hearts. God does such a beautiful job of taking those exclamations and etching them into the students' spiritual memories. All we have to do is offer an avenue for the ah-ha's to be uttered.

MILE MARKER THIS...

Site D.I.G.S.

One of my favorite youth ministry resources is a book called *On Site: 40 On-Location Youth Programs* by Rick Bundschuh.[12] It has great ideas for taking students to unconventional places like a trash dump for a lesson on the garbage we pile up in our lives or to the viewing window in a hospital's infant nursery to illustrate Psalm 139. ("For you created my inmost being; you knit me together in my mother's womb. I praise you because I am fearfully and wonderfully made; your works are wonderful, I know that full well" (vv. 13-14).) On-site learning experiences make a strong memory about Scripture truth and application in our lives.

Bread Making

Illustrate several scriptural lessons by making bread either in front of or with adolescents. You can focus on Jesus as the Bread of Life (John 6:25-59), good yeast versus bad yeast (Galatians 5), or how God can shape and edify us to sustain others through adversity (kneading). If you don't think you can pull off the bread making yourself, invite a friend with some dough experience to make it for you or show students how to make it while you facilitate the lesson or conversation.

The Problem Station

Create a problem station in a place that's visible and where students can often stop and contemplate a possible life struggle, community issue, or global crisis. Make the backdrop big and intriguing so it invites them into the problem. Consider putting a particular problem up for a whole month and ask individual students or small groups to spend some time reading through the information, studying the pictures, and committing regular times of thought and prayer to what a Christ-follower's response should be. Create a blog or online discussion group to give students a forum for working through the problem and a place where they can invite their friends to join in.

Reasons to Believe

Create a mile marker journal or box that you can give to your students early in their adolescent experience. Include a sturdy piece of paper or a small cardboard box with a slit in the top. At the top of the paper or somewhere on the box, title it REASONS TO BELIEVE and remind students throughout their junior high or high school years to make a list of all the reasons they find to believe in God and trust him to lead their lives during their adolescence. If they've already created a list, they can just add a new reason or two each year. If they have a mile marker box, then they can write the new reason on a scrap of paper and slide it into the box. At a celebration sometime later in their adolescent journey, give them a chance to share some of the reasons that made it onto their list.

DIG GOD'S STORY

At the risk of sounding too retro, students need to really "dig" the Story of God. They certainly need to know it, hear it, and remember it. But their knowledge will morph into experience if they not only know the Story, but also appreciate it, cherish it, stand in awe of it, and are transformed by it. When those verbs start happening in their spiritual lives, we can celebrate the fact that they're experiencing the power of the Story.

Amazing Information

My first seminary professor was Dr. Art Patzia. The class was New Testament II, which focused on the book of Acts through the book of Revelation. That class transformed how I pictured the early church, which in turn reshaped my personal studies of the epistles, which eventually impacted how I communicated the story and truth of those books. Dr. Patzia wasn't content to have us understand the story. He fervently drew the picture of the world in which the story occurred. He connected the dots of how the history lessons of my youth lined up with the events in the first century church. He took us through a thorough exploration of Roman culture and religious practices that stunned me. Suddenly, Paul's words to the people of Athens in Acts 17 came to life as I considered their honest search for a God they could know and who could know them.

Within this historical and cultural framework, our class weighed the meaning of these letters written to the early believers. We knew they were God's words entrusted to the voice and pen of a person, so we considered what we already knew about God's character and history in earlier Scriptures to cast light on our studies. Most of us hadn't had any classes in Greek yet. But Dr. Patzia still helped us think through the language that was used and appreciate the richness and depth of meaning behind the English translation.

And finally, each day Dr. Patzia would joyfully assign a ridiculous amount of reading for the next class. What we didn't know—as we groaned about the hours we'd spend reading before the class met again—was that we'd be repeatedly saying things like, "Wow!" or, "I didn't know that!" as we read. It was impossible to miss his enthusiasm and the way this subject permeated his own life. For many of us, his love for the story he shared was contagious. And the few students who didn't always appreciate his teaching style certainly didn't forget the experience.

Very few of our students will attend a Christian college or seminary, so why not breathe some life back into the confirmation class by taking young teenagers on a scriptural adventure? Why not lead a Bible study with such energy and exuberance that our students wonder what's wrong with us? Why not surprise them with a theological wondering in the middle of a pick-up basketball game and unpack it later? Why not invite a little controversy by working a spiritual paradox that's often explained away in our churches into a conversation over coffee? Among the many lessons I learned from Dr. Patzia is the one he taught me about how the essence of talking to students about God's Story involves checking my ho-hum attitude at the door and opening my mouth with the confidence that God will renovate a student's life.

Mystical Moments

For some leaders, talking and teaching about Scripture comes naturally. The words resonate on their hearts, and they know how to convey the power and truth found on the pages of Scripture. Over the years, I've gradually learned to look for the unseen movements of God in the stories of the past and present, too. To me, the most important word in Hebrews 4:12 is the word *is*. God's Word wasn't alive at one time. It is alive. It is still working. It still has a heartbeat. It's still a lifeline. And if it's alive and powerful, then I shouldn't be surprised to experience some of the mystery that comes with it.

Oftentimes, my students remind me of the mystical side of our faith. Fortunately for youth ministry leaders, adolescents tend to be more open to mystical experiences than adults are. And in a broader sense, our culture is very open to mysticism now, which certainly helps us show students the things they cannot see.

One of my college students came back from a summer in Egypt and told me of many instances when people approached him and asked if he could tell them about Jesus. It's important to know this young man has blonde hair and blue eyes, so an Egyptian man would easily assume him to be a Westerner and a Christian. The wonder part of his story was that every one of these people had experienced a dream in which Jesus spoke to them.

It occurred to me that the experiences these people had in their dreams would most likely be dismissed as not being real or valid in our Western Christian culture. For the most part, it seems we've become too academic in our pursuit of God today. Information is crucial, but so is the connection to our psyche.

Students will naturally go to a place of spiritual connectedness if we not only encourage and guide them, but also are careful not to diminish or explain away any movements of God that they may sense in their lives. The worst thing we could do in this situation is deflate their soul's sensitivity by saying that miracles no longer happen, God doesn't speak in dreams, and there's nothing extraordinary happening in our world anymore (even though we worship an extraordinary God). There's a difference between someone incorrectly proclaiming a new revelation from God and correctly recognizing the revelation that our God is still alive and at work!

The Self and the Selfless

There is an uncommon beauty in a person's walk with God. It's the paradox that it's very much meant for us individually, and at the same time it's not about us at all. It's the joint reality of finding oneself and giving oneself away. Scripture captures our souls with the promises of a God who knows us and loves us, right down to the number of seconds we'll live and the number of cells in our bodies. God knows us from the inside out; God watches over our comings and goings in daily living, and God extended himself into humanity to draw us back into his presence. God is actively participating in each of our lives in an intimate way.

Students need this message echoing throughout their adolescent journey. Oftentimes they're surrounded by adults, but they don't feel as though very many grown-ups are on their side. There are days when they don't know who is looking out for them, and they feel invisible to the busy, preoccupied adults in their lives. So students need a reminder that they were never meant to travel their life's road alone. They need moments when they know God is present and focused on them.

At the same time, students also need to understand that faith in Jesus is a journey into selflessness. Our experience of God's presence in our lives is intended to prompt us to come alongside others and share what we've received, just like John and Emily did by teaching middle school students drawing and paintings at our summer art camp, or how Blake and Jeff showed up every Sunday morning for three years to lead their high school peers in worship. It's a faith that grows stale and brittle without sacrifice. Grace begets compassion. Mercy births forgiveness. Strength offers encouragement. What students receive through that Divine-human exchange is best internalized when they offer it to others who also need to know they're not alone.

MILE MARKER THIS...

What Does Lent and Ash Have to Do With It?

I once heard a simple explanation of Lent that had a profound impact on me. The speaker talked about the purpose of mourning the death of Christ before celebrating his resurrection. It was a message about turning from darkness to light and literally turning our back on a life of ashes. That was the first time that many of our students and youth workers heard Lent described in a way that brought meaning to the relevance of its practice.

So the next time you realize that Easter is only a few months away, consider planning some kind of Ash Wednesday experience where students don't just recite a prayer and have ashes smeared on their foreheads without really understanding the exercise. Make it a turn-around, light-and-dark gathering about the next 40 days of their lives, during which they'll contemplate all of the biblical stories in which someone endured for 40 days, wandered for 40 years, or was resurrected after 40 hours. Make sure you challenge your students to give more of themselves to God, give deeper devotion to living intentionally, and give up more for the sake of others during those days.

Patriarch Sitcom Montage

The patriarchs of the Old Testament were both phenomenal leaders and deeply flawed humans. At first glance, some of their antics are almost laughable. That's why there's a ton of good sitcom material that illustrates the bumblings and mishaps of the Hebrew founding fathers. Study the story of Abraham, Jacob, or any of Jacob's sons and decide which sitcoms most appropriately and honestly reflect the kinds of family situations that exist in these biblical narratives. Then put together a video montage of clips that translate the situations well and let students guess which patriarchal story each sitcom clip represents. This is a great launching point for talking about these heroes of the faith and reminding your students that the heroes' greatness came from God. Finish by letting students discuss or journal about the connections between their families and those who lived thousands of years ago. If you have the people, talent, and creativity, you could do your own homegrown Monty Python type of spoof of the patriarchal stories.

Big God, Small World

Set up a video conference call to a group of adolescent believers in another country and let them report to their Western peers all that God is doing in their world. Gather stories of miraculous occurrences and appearances from around the world. You may even know someone who's encountered God working in a dynamic way somewhere else in the world. Let this person share the story with your students. If you don't know a first-person source, then find some stories online via Web sites for mission organizations and churches overseas. This global faith experience can ignite students' excitement for expecting God to do great things around them.

Questions to Ask at the Most Random Moments

Surprise students every so often by asking them a random question that's ripe with meaning. Ask a middle school student why God chose to make the sky blue and not red. Or ask a high school guy what his initial gut response would be if his girlfriend became pregnant after they had sex only two times. Or maybe ask a high school girl why Jesus needed friends if he was God. These can't be ambush questions where the student feels trapped and unable to answer. Instead, these are more like "What do you think?" kinds of questions that are meant to keep students contemplating toward a life-shaping answer, rather than guessing at what they think is the right one.

Taken, Blessed, Broken, Given

Using the idea found in Eugene Peterson's book *The Jesus Way*, lead adolescents through a cycle of experiences that represent being taken, being blessed, being broken, and being given.[13] It can be prayer stations that illustrate how the act of Communion is connected to the whole of our lives, or it could be a series of days or weeks in which all that we do in our ministry gatherings is reenact and recognize real-time moments of being taken, blessed, broken, and given.

EXIT RAMP

Without sharing any of the ideas that might be in this book, I asked some of my student alums to share their good, bad, and ugly experiences at Redeemer. I found these thoughts from a young professional named Kristin to be fitting for keeping the spiritual conversations going:

> The message we got at Redeemer was a message of truth but also a message of grace and God's extravagant love for us. [Students] will need that message drilled into them over and over again. We knew the truth. We talked about truth, we talked about the Word, and, most importantly, we talked about the importance of a personal walk with the Lord.

I wholeheartedly encourage youth workers to have a plan, a vision, and a structure to their student ministry. They're tools that keep us effective and focused in ministry. But in the midst of planning and organizing, you can't go wrong by weaving in the real and figurative conversations about following Christ. In all of Kristin's thoughts, she didn't once mention a revolutionary event that set her on the right path, but only her conversations with trusted adult mentors along her adolescent road that made all the difference.

1. Where are the students you know on their respective faith journeys?

2. Where do they need to go?

3. What are your initial thoughts for how to help them get there?

Mileage Reminders and Celebrations

"Tie them to your hands and wear them on your forehead as reminders. Write them on the doorposts of your house and on your gates."
Deuteronomy 6:8-9 (NLT)

CHAPTER

8

When my ministry time with the students at Redeemer Covenant Church neared its end, I wanted to leave the girls with a lasting imprint of the community they were now a part of. We invited high school girls and former female students from the last 13 years to join us for a catered dinner at a student's home. We also invited all of the current and past female leaders to attend. Each table contained a mix of high school girls, college and career women, young moms, and female mentors—all of whom had either grown up in our student ministry or served as leaders. They ate together, talked, laughed, shared stories, and poked fun at me. (There's lots of material on that subject!)

After dinner I had them gather around for the most uncomfortable picture they've probably ever taken. They were instructed to reach out one hand onto the floor of the foyer and place it near the cross that lay in the center. Then we took the picture.

Next, I gave a short message on how they're each part of a spiritual legacy of women who came before them and the girls who will come after them. Then each woman received a framed black-and-white print of the picture we'd taken earlier. All that can be seen in the photograph is the hands of dozens of girls and women, all reaching to touch the cross at the center.

If you look closely at the picture, you can see the small hand of one extra guest. It's my daughter Lanie's hand. I brought her with me that night because so many of those girls had left an imprint on her life. She was a much-loved tag-a-long in our community, and it seemed fitting to include her—for her sake and for theirs. And that's what I wanted to make sure they remembered that night—how our shared belief in Christ and the overlapping days of our shared journeys have changed us, and we should continue the legacy of letting it change others.

So we tell the stories, we massage them into students' lives, and then we put reminders along their paths to help them remember not only the stories, but how they were changed and strengthened by them, too. If I ask a student to summarize the main point of a lesson I taught last month, chances are good that she's forgotten it. But if I give her a tangible or experiential reminder, she'll carry and recall that truth a long way down the road.

HANDS, FOREHEADS, HOUSES, AND GATES

Not long ago, I watched a segment on the evening news about rites of passage practices around the world. One of the stories was about a young Jewish teenager who was wearing a tassel tied to his hand and a box attached to his forehead. I'd been reading about this ritual and was thrilled to see that thousands of years after the words in Deuteronomy were written, the simple ancient practice still had a place in our media-saturated world.

The Jewish faithful tied tassels, called tzitzits, to their hands and garments as reminders of God's directions for their lives. They'd also copy Scripture passages onto small pieces of paper and put them inside little boxes (called tefillin or phylacteries) as a reminder to keep God's Word close to their hearts and minds. These actions didn't make them more spiritual, righteous people. They merely served as practical, visible reminders of the road they'd chosen and the destination they were striving for.

When I talk to a former student of mine 20 years from now, I hope he remembers the "tassels" we gave him to tie to his garments so he'd remember who he is and Whose he is. That tassel could be a funny T-shirt from a fall retreat or mission project. It could be the gripping cross he received at a prayer labyrinth walk. It might be the study Bible he received after he spent a year studying the Old and New Testaments in our Journey program. It might also be the Letter from God that we sent to him and he hung on his bedroom mirror where he'd see it every morning.[14] Regardless of which item it is, my hope is that he remembers the gift box of truth that he opened again and again to discover a lifetime of strength, hope, and purpose that would easily outlast the few miles that the other youth ministry leaders and I got to travel with him on his journey.

Signs and Symbols—Something to Hold Onto

For two days all I could think was, How do I explain the Trinity to these middle school kids? I struggled to come up with a tangible illustration to explain an intangible concept. And then I finally reached back into my very limited scientific background and thought of one option. It wasn't a perfect analogy, but the basics of it certainly worked. In a little Ziploc baggie, I put an ice cube and a little water, and then I left room for a little air. In class, we talked about how God the Father, God the Son, and God the Spirit were made up of the same spiritual elements but functioned in different forms. Of course, I offered the disclaimer that the air inside the baggie was actually more than just evaporated H_2O, but there was still some invisible evaporated water present, too. We spent time discussing how all three forms were still H_2O, yet at the same time, each had appeared in a different shape.

How often do we read a passage of Scripture in which God gives a person a tangible reminder of what he's done? He gave Jacob a physical injury when they wrestled. And it's quite possible that God was saying, "Jacob, your inner strength is incredible, but don't forget that I'm stronger." And who could forget watching a small sea of water divide right before their eyes as it allowed them to cross to the other side and escape the dangers behind them?

Jesus offered these kinds of reminders all the time. I can just imagine Jesus holding up a staff as he talked about being the Good Shepherd. It's possible he passed around a flask of water to share as he spoke of being the Living Water. And he probably picked a brilliantly sunny day to proclaim that he was the light that would enter human hearts and save the world. Jesus used physical blindness—via a brilliant light—to reveal to Paul his own spiritual blindness, and Jesus didn't restore Paul's sight until his soul saw things more clearly. This symbol of Paul's brokenness and unbelief became Paul's reminder to follow hard after Christ all the rest of his days.

The signs and symbols we give to our students can be simple, homemade, and inexpensive. I've observed a student carrying around a 10-cent wooden pocket cross that he's had for years. They can also be elaborate and a bit pricey. We wanted our students' Bibles to offer tools to help them with prayer and study. So our Senior Banquet budget line item for the seniors' gifts—a lightweight study Bible they could take along to college or wherever their lives took them—was usually the largest portion of the entire event's expenses.

For the guys' rite of passage event at Redeemer (see chapter 6), we gave students a knife with the words WHEN I BECAME A MAN… inscribed in Greek along the handle. The leaders wanted to mark the day when each ninth grade guy began walking around the lake with his father and thinking about his life from the perspective of a boy, and ended that pivotal journey while thinking about his identity as a man.

We can give students a gift that reflects all that God has given to us, like the homegrown CD our student musicians made. We paid for the recording, reproduction, and copyright licenses so our high school students who'd devoted so much time to playing and singing for our worship times could enjoy the recording experience. Then we gave a free copy to all of our students. For the majority of our student ministry, it was a wonderful reminder of the powerful times of worship we shared together. For the musicians, it was another form of encouragement and served as an affirmation of their giftedness in an arena where adults usually get more leadership opportunities.

It's fun for students to walk away from some new place we've taken them with a souvenir that reminds them of why we went there, like the Noah's Ark T-shirts we bought after students braved the Arkansas River rapids, climbed and rappelled Bob's Rock, and spent two days and nights on a peak climb on our first Colorado Adventure trip. Or when we've shared a significant experience together, they can carry that memory with them in the form of a memento, like the little pieces of old rags that students traded for a small, white, new cloth that we gave them after a midnight Easter service where they'd just experienced the power of Walter Wangerin's Ragman story.[15]

These kinds of "tassels and boxes" don't represent the essence of the lesson or experience that we want students to receive. Instead, they're reminders of the essence of God's character and participation in their lives. They're one way of helping God's Story leap from the pages of Scripture into their immediate daily living.

Driving Stakes in the Ground—Something to Do

When I met Gundy, Drew, Mick, Grant, Rem, and Jeff, they were a bunch of freshman guys who didn't talk a lot and didn't seek out attention. I didn't know their stories, but that would change over the course of the next four years.

I believe what brought them together initially was track. They all competed in some track event, and most of them ran cross-country. I remember the first time they showed up for the state meet with bleached-blonde hair. They were a force to be reckoned with on the field, and this show of unity was a visible reminder to their opponents. They almost always arrived together, especially before they started driving. And there was always a ripple in the dynamics of the room when they entered. I eventually understood that ripple to be a wave of admiration from their peers.

They all came from very different life experiences, and I watched and marveled as their friendships with one another strengthened throughout high school. They became a spiritual band of brothers who rallied for each other to succeed, challenged each other in big and small things, and stuck together in the worst of times.

According to Mick, one simple high school tradition made all the difference in his adolescent pilgrimage: A Prayer Triplet exercise during an Easter devotional week called Walk to the Cross. Between Palm Sunday and Easter, students read devotions written by other students and our adult leaders, and they gathered for personal and community experiences to reflect on the Passion.

During Prayer Triplets, students were encouraged to gather with at least two other friends in a quiet space and spend time in prayer for themselves, each other, and their world. So one evening Mick, Drew, Gundy, Grant, Rem, and Jeff all gathered at a park to pray. According to Mick, they had no clue what they were doing, but they gave it a shot. I knew these guys met for the Prayer Triplet experience. What I didn't know was that night was only the beginning of a weekly gathering of prayer, sharing, and accountability between these typically quiet, unassuming guys. They were just a group of high school guys walking the tough road of adolescence together and searching for direction and purpose. And they met that way throughout most of high school.

Mick described it as the "stake in the ground" for his spiritual journey as an adolescent. It became the pivotal experience for him to deepen his walk with God and understand his purpose. For Gundy, the event of something like Prayer Triplets wasn't the catalyst for his transformation, it was the friendships he shared with these guys that he remembers as being life-changing:

I don't think of moments in my life, while participating at Redeemer, where the actual event was the thing that caused a big difference. To me, the biggest factor in high school was my friend base. They were the people I looked to for help, encouragement, and discipleship when I was a young Christian. Now, even though I don't recall specific events being the factor, every event I remember helped in continuing and furthering those bonds between me and my friends. Redeemer was a good place, a safe place, where many felt they had the opportunity to speak their mind about God and receive good and constructive listening and feedback. I think it was that mentality that rubbed off on us the most. As I look at my friends now, I can see that we have all been moved and changed by the ethos that was at Redeemer, not really an event.

There are huge endeavors that we youth leaders work on to help students hammer a marker of maturity somewhere along their path. And then there are the underestimated small things that resonate with the same force in their lives. Whether the plan is modest or bombastic, the goal should be to give them something they can come back to often, either in remembrance or practice.

Stranded Travelers—Someone to Help

One Friday night I got a phone call from a student of mine named Elizabeth, and she had a wonderfully surprising question to ask me. She and a friend had just finished eating dinner at a local restaurant, and they'd encountered a seemingly homeless woman sitting on a public bench with all of her belongings in a shopping cart. It's important to note that Elizabeth had recently gone on an urban mission project with a team from our student ministry to Center for Student Missions (CSM). During that trip, they'd served in soup kitchens, food agencies, and childcare centers mostly in Houston's Fifth Ward district. And this phone call came several weeks after we'd arrived home from that trip. Elizabeth's question was whether or not she should do something to help the woman.

We talked about what she'd be able to do as a 16-year-old without a lot of money on hand and no adult support nearby. And then Elizabeth decided it would be appropriate for her to offer this woman something for warmth, since it was a chilly night. So Elizabeth and her friend bought the woman a hot chocolate and sat down to visit with her while she waited for the bus. Now, I've known Elizabeth for a long time, and I knew she had a compassionate heart. But I believe that trip to Houston (where she practiced serving people in need from 6 A.M. to 10 P.M. every day for a week) had prepared her for just such a moment at home. I also believe that because she entered a world of strangers who loved and engaged her, even though their life circumstances were vastly different from hers, she was changed by the stories they shared with her.

Our youth ministry's first CSM trip was to Washington D.C. And I have to admit that back then, I was still on a learning curve regarding the impact of mission experiences for students. I approached the planning of it from the perspective of how our students could make a difference. But what I love about CSM is that they just quietly allow the mission experience to transform the hearts of those who serve. So I was learning valuable truth and receiving preparation for a new way of living right along with my students.

When we returned home from that five-day trip, a handful of students who'd served breakfast together at Third Street Church of God and delivered meals to homebound HIV patients decided the work should continue at home. Without much help or input from me, they contacted the DayCenter for the Homeless in Tulsa and signed up to prepare, deliver, and serve dinner to approximately 100 people once a month for most of the next two years. They came up with a menu, organized food sign-ups with students and adults, recruited a team to go serve, and then came ready to not only serve dinner on those evenings, but also spend time talking and sharing with the DayCenter clients. Since my only real job was driving the lead vehicle, sometimes I'd have to drag students away from their conversations because we were already 20 minutes late in leaving for home.

In a world where our culture almost always tells students and adults to consider themselves first, ministry is completely inadequate without some stops along the road where students have the opportunity to walk and talk with a stranded traveler. The experience of intersecting their lives with the journeys of others who have different perspectives and needs is probably one of the best ways to help students really understand themselves and see the face of someone else's struggle. The cost of such giving and understanding will reshape their cultural paradigm of "me."

Off-Road Adventures—Somewhere New to Visit.

You may have already picked up on a nuance between my beloved spouse and me. He's the planner and I'm...not! I must admit that over the years I've learned a lot from him about planning things—everything from handling our finances to organizing the pantry. (Actually, I drew the line at his pantry rearrangements.) But my favorite part of the Gary McKinney planning feature of our marriage is the family vacations. Our family has seen more interesting off-the-beaten-path sights and done more unique and memorable things together because he researches things to do months before a trip.

Before we had kids, a random stop on a road trip was just for the fun of exploration. We've had a band of aggressive monkeys beat on our windshield when we tried to feed them cheese curls at a drive-through safari park. (I guess you aren't supposed to do that!) We also spent a day exploring the mountains and deserts of California by following wherever the road took us.

But when the kids came along, stopping along the road for a breather every once in a while became a necessity. So now Gary puts together a notebook of all kinds of interesting roadside attractions and distractions that we keep in the front seat. On the way to wherever we're going, if the moment should arise—and it often does—that someone needs a bathroom break or a recess from car constraints, we pull out the notebook and see what little off-road adventure we can have. Most of the time, it's a potential break that was part of Gary's overall plan. But sometimes we'll spot a billboard that calls our names, and we trek a few miles off the highway to go have some fun. The trip is certainly longer this way, but it's more fun for everyone.

We've made some pretty wonderful memories during our impromptu stops. Lanie learned how to cross the monkey bars for the first time at a rest stop in Texas. This year, we hiked to the top of the Capulin Volcano National Monument near Raton, New Mexico, on our way home from Colorado. From the highest point on the rim, we could see the plains and mountains of three states. Not all sidebar trips are a monumental success, but even a less-than-impressive roadside attraction is usually good material for some memories.

I found Gary's style of planning (in this instance) to be very transferable to my ministry paradigm. We often take students on road trips and adventures in youth ministry. Sometimes it's a real trip. Other times, it's a weekly attempt to take them somewhere in their hearts and minds. Either type of excursion can benefit from a stash of off-road ideas just in case students need a breather.

On a real trip, it's a lot like our family's ramblings. There's a plan for getting to our destination, but we include a few options for stopping should we need to break up the miles. Our willingness to make an impromptu stop may prove to build some stronger memories than the original plan. And when we want to take our students to a different place without leaving the room, the same idea applies. We have a creative overall plan and a few back-up options in case we need to change gears. But then, every so often, students should have the opportunity to show up and have all of their expectations challenged. Surprise is still a powerful element in teaching and leading—as long as the surprise is for the good of the students and not to humor the adult leaders.

ROADSIDE ASSISTANCE—SOMEDAY WHEN HELP IS NEEDED

One morning I received a startling email from a friend of a college student. She wanted me to email her friend and inquire about a pretty big life situation that she was facing. So I emailed this college student, whom I'd known since she was in eighth grade, and I quickly discovered she was pregnant and had made an appointment to have an abortion the next morning. She wanted to talk to me, but she didn't. She was so torn and scared that it seemed she couldn't think clearly. I tried to keep the communication lines open all day and evening—all the while praying fervently for her heart and mind to be protected from all the distress she was feeling. I knew this wasn't the choice she wanted to make, but she felt trapped and ashamed. She was afraid to face her friends and family. I was awake most of the night praying for her, even though I couldn't reach her.

The next morning I contemplated whether or not I should try to intervene. I didn't want to break the trust between this young woman and her parents, but I also felt I should try one more time to reach her. So I drove to her neighborhood and parked down the street from her house. I spent about 20 minutes praying for her, and then I called the house. Her mom answered, but I didn't feel it was my place to say something to her mom. So I asked to speak with her daughter. The mom knew who I was, and she added my 8 A.M. call to a list of other odd occurrences over the past few days.

The girl and I spoke briefly, and I assured her that no matter what she decided, I was still going to care for her. I also reminded her that this wasn't the only option and that God has this amazing ability to redeem the difficulties in our lives for good, even the ones we bring upon ourselves. She thanked me and that was the end of the conversation.

> In a world where our culture almost always tells students and adults to consider themselves first, ministry is completely inadequate without some stops along the road where students have the opportunity to walk and talk with a stranded traveler.

Later that morning, her mom called me. She'd put all the pieces together and decided something serious was going on with her daughter. So when her daughter got out of the shower, her mom walked into her room and asked her if she was pregnant. That was all she needed to change her mind. Getting past the hurdle of having to tell her parents and not having to hide the situation anymore was the release and strength she needed to cancel that appointment.

It might be a car wreck or a suicide attempt. It could be a meth party or a gang initiation. It might be an abusive home or an accidental death. For one youth ministry friend, it was a student who stabbed another teenager at a weekend party. By Monday morning, the young man had been charged with murder. My friend John dropped everything he'd planned and spent the week trying to get into the facility where the student was being held. Even if he got only a few moments with the student, John wanted to remind him that he wasn't alone, nor was he rejected.

Our students face far more tragedies on the road to adolescence than they should ever have to. It might be their fault or someone else's. There may be an arrest or just a lifetime of guilt to battle. We may have the perfect Scripture for the moment, or we may not have a clue as to what we should say. It doesn't matter what the destruction has been. Students need adults who are willing to offer that roadside assistance and get to them wherever they are in the turmoil. And in those moments it really doesn't matter if we have the perfect words to say. It only matters that we go.

MILE MARKER THIS...

Add an H to the Name

In the Jewish faith, there are prayers like the Elohai N'shamah where there are so many "h" and "ah" sounds that a person cannot help but hear herself breathe as she speaks the words of the prayer.[16] That breath is a powerful reminder of the life God breathed into each of us. So sometime during a pivotal gathering or rite of passage, offer students a gift that has their name inscribed into it, but with an H added in. This is the symbol of God giving them life and purpose, and it's also a reminder to find hope in that breath each time they hear or speak it.

Footwashing

Most people have never participated in a footwashing service, yet it has the potential to immediately usher participants back two thousand years to the most symbolic and agonizing night of Jesus' life. It's the act where they feel with their own big toe what true selflessness is. It's the reminder of the humility that should permeate our lives. It's a scary experience for anyone at first, but to gather a group of students on a patio or—better yet—in an upper room to relive these crucial moments in Jesus' life and the lives of his disciples is to connect them to an ancient, but ever-renewing legacy. All that's needed are a few candles, a bowl, a pitcher of water, some towels, and the passage from John 13. Do a quick demonstration, and then allow each person to wash the feet of the person beside him. That way everyone washes and gets washed. Later, individuals can seek out special friends and leaders to wash their feet.

Candles on the Cross

One year, instead of practicing our traditional "nailing our sins" to the cross at a midnight Easter service, we glued small votive candles (with metal bases) all over a wooden cross while we talked about Jesus being the light. At the end of the service, students were invited to come to the cross, light a candle, and spend time in prayer. The mixture of sadness and joy over all that Jesus gave up on our behalf was visualized on a splintery wooden cross that gradually became full of light.

THE BEGINNING, THE MIDDLE, AND THE END

In a practice similar to the personal reminders of tassels and boxes, the Jewish people were commanded to write reminders of the Law in plain sight on their gates and doorposts. As they headed out into the world, the words on the gate reminded them to cling to the promises that had been planted in their hearts. And whenever they returned home, the inscriptions on the doorposts clearly and immediately reminded them of the hope that held them.

A few years ago, I trained for and ran the Oklahoma City Memorial Half-Marathon. I'm not a fast runner, but I've always run to keep in shape. My husband had run the 13-mile event the previous year, and he encouraged me that it would be amazing. So I did it. If you've ever run a long-distance event like that, then you know what a grueling, yet inspiring, experience it is. What stood out to me as being the best surprises of the run, however, were the beginning, the middle, and the end. Yes, that's right, because at 6:30 a.m., they made a huge deal about the thousands of people who were lined up at the starting line. Speeches were made by civic leaders, accolades were given to all the runners and even some live music was played to fire us up. Then, all along the course, there were corporate-sponsored refreshment stations, live music, and crowds of cheering strangers. It was like a little party for my tired body and spirit every half-mile.

And at the finish line was the biggest party of all—a festival complete with tons of free food to replenish our strength, carnival games, and another live concert. Even though I could barely lift my legs to step onto a curb, the moment I crossed that finish line I felt like I could conquer anything!

We must remember that this adolescent marathon needs some party stations along the course, too. It's really important to make sure we help kids do a lot of celebrating throughout these years, not just at the end. Proclamations, preparation, and celebrations can all be the gate and doorpost inscriptions for our students. Teenagers need us to acknowledge when they stand at the edge of something new and momentous. They need cheerleaders and coaches and refreshment in the middle of experiences that are no longer new, but aren't yet finished. They need support when they're tired and thinking about quitting. And finally, they need a huge party at the finish line. Every celebration reinforces the lessons and truths they've encountered on their journey.

Anticipation

You might've seen the Disney "Anticipation" commercial where the little brother and sister can't go to sleep because they're leaving for Disney World the next morning. After the mom has firmly told the kids to go to sleep, she climbs back into bed and asks the dad if he's asleep. He replies, "No, I'm too excited."

One of the most important exercises we can do with students is help them savor the anticipation for their adolescent journey. It's important for them to witness adults helping them look forward to the miles that lie ahead, rather than the typical worry and sarcasm they usually get. It isn't a trip for the faint of heart, but it can be a magnificent journey through the mountains and the valleys. And having a guide who is excited for them sure helps. Anticipation is an easy goal to achieve as long as it's not an afterthought in planning. Obviously, if we don't anticipate it, then we can't help them anticipate it!

In our community students exit elementary school and enter an intermediate campus in fifth grade. Many then move on to actual middle school in seventh grade and high school in ninth. The whole idea that they spend four years being either an "intermediate" or "middle" school student is not a title that inspires enthusiasm. Who wants to be stuck in the middle for four years?

I've often heard moms of fifth grade students say that their kids really miss elementary school. That surprised me at first, but then I thought about how much a middle schooler's life, body, relationships, and responsibilities change without all of the fanfare they enjoy in high school. So our ministry should have some intentional next-level anticipation built into the segues between elementary school, middle school, and high school.

How we anticipate with our students depends on what our ministry looks like and how we're connected to them. The goal for this kind of anticipation is to make sure they feel known, invited, and understood at the beginning. It's also to demonstrate to them that we're thrilled for them and have some knowledge and encouragement to offer as they embark on a new road.

It's important to discern between anticipatory events and hazing blunders. I learned this the hard way many years ago when I very naïvely let our senior class organize the ninth grade welcome event without a lot of adult guidance. Every time I turned around, an upperclassman was crossing the line from celebration to humiliation. Their goal was to put the freshman class in their place. The activities they'd planned weren't terrible ideas, but the spirit and purpose behind them were certainly aggressive. There are still students from that freshman class who can now lightheartedly share how that event skewed them about youth ministry life at Redeemer for a while.

So I put a few rules in place to avoid such a discouraging occurrence again. First, if it requires getting dirty and gross, then everyone participates in the dirtiness and the grossness. Second, a new freshman can always opt out if she feels uncomfortable. Third, the goal is to make their younger peers excited for the months to come, not to fire them up to do the same thing to next year's freshmen. Lastly, a new freshman should leave the event admiring the upperclassmen and having made a few "got your back" friends among them, not thinking less of them and feeling anxious about returning. I realize there are questionable initiation practices in all kinds of clubs, fraternities, and groups that students will aspire to join. But in the community of Christ followers, initiation should only be intended to invite, welcome, and initiate something new and good into their lives.

Anticipation doesn't just have to be event-driven. It can be personal and very specific to a person or a small group of students. We had a wonderfully generous owner of a local Arby's franchise who donated free meal coupons that we could give to our students for their birthdays. I never knew I could make a student's day with a little meal card and a homemade birthday greeting. But time and again, I'd receive emails and texts from students who couldn't believe we'd paid attention to their birthday and given them a little something at that! That small celebration in an envelope told them we knew what age milestone was upon them and we cared about where they were on their journey.

Another time, a group of students were performing in *A Midsummer Night's Dream*. I just happened to stumble upon the perfect memento to wish them well in their performance. While walking through Yankee Candle Company, I spotted a candle aptly named "Midsummer's Night." I purchased enough for each of our students in the production, as well as a few extras for their friends whom I'd met a few times. I think I added a note about them shining brightly on the stage and, of course, that they should break a leg. Hopefully, that small gift boosted their excitement for their opening performance and also communicated that my care for their lives encompassed not only their spiritual identity, but also extracurricular things like drama productions.

Preparation

With the anticipation we build for our students, we then need to equip them for the journey ahead. It's wonderful to kindle their excitement for the miles they're about to travel. But if they don't have the proper instruction and gear, then they won't have nearly as much fun walking the road. The journey that's meant to be an adventure into adulthood can suddenly become a train wreck in the middle of nowhere. So they need opportunities to get ready, to build their endurance for the difficult hikes, and to learn where to look for help when it's needed.

Preparation can be a rite of passage, a unique group study and discussion, or even a weekly one-on-one contact over coffee. It can look like a homegrown devotional gift, a retreat about moving on or intimate relationships, or breakout sessions about issues they'll face in college (led by those who've gone before them). Once again, it's about taking a look at the students we lead and asking ourselves what they need to grow and thrive in the coming days. How can we prepare them for what lies ahead?

One issue I keep seeing in the news is how adolescents aren't prepared to manage their finances when they leave high school or college. That's something my husband knows a lot about, since he spent four years as a financial consultant. Healthy finances are something he's also passionate about living and modeling for others. So whether it's a group of high school seniors who need several weeks of training on money matters, or a college student who's trying to get his finances in order before graduation, Gary is the person I connect them with because I know he cares about the subject and the application of the advice he offers.

There are also lots of reclaim and redeem possibilities in this arena of preparation. I've often thought that instead of the usual jokes about getting off the road because a 16-year-old just got her license, maybe a great preparation for the future driving she'll be doing would be a small License to Drive party. During this gathering she could hear a variety of driving disaster stories and gentle advice from adults who care about her. Surrounded by her friends, food, and music, the one-hour mini-celebration then concludes with everyone praying a special blessing over this new privilege and responsibility in her life. With such an important mile marker, we want her to sense our confidence that she's capable and ready, not our certainty that she'll total the car within a week.

Mileage Has Its Rewards

We travel through Missouri a few times a year to visit my grandmother. Not long before I began this writing project, we were on our way to see Grandma in Bethany, and I noticed something I'd never paid attention to before. The mile markers in Missouri mark not only each mile, but also every tenth of a mile. No joke. Just in case I'm not sure how far I've gone or where I am on the highway, I have the assurance of those little green signs marking my location and progress. Gary and I both commented on what a huge endeavor and expense those signs must have been for the state of Missouri. We wondered about the people who'd made those tenth-of-a-mile signs a priority.

Part of the pain that goes along with traveling the long adolescent road comes from students growing weary and losing steam or not recognizing they've made progress in their sense of identity and spiritual maturity. Although I'm not sure that cars traveling 70 miles an hour need to be reminded that they've gone yet another 528 feet, I do believe the tenth-of-a-mile rule is brilliant for the adolescent pilgrimage. Students need to receive notes, mini-parties, recognition, rewards, free food, surprise gifts, relevant books, homemade CDs, Facebook gifts, and timely text messages in order to trust that they've grown and succeeded. They need to be reminded of their potential and strength quite often—especially when they're in that middle zone. It wouldn't surprise me at all to learn that for some students, their very adolescent survival is dependent on small incidents of encouragement that all connect together to form a safety net in their lives—a safety net that keeps them from faltering.

MILE MARKER THIS...

Name Celebration

Research what your students' names mean and share with them how you see the meaning of their names being demonstrated in their lives. It's amazing how much each of us lives the legacy of our name, if even just a little bit. Throw this mini-celebration for a small group, with a son or daughter, or with a larger crowd if you've got the time and resources to include everyone. You can also put their pictures, their names, and their names' meanings in a video and use it with a lesson about the meanings behind the names of people mentioned in Scripture.

Travelogue

This is a diary of sorts, but it can be written, visual, metaphorical—you name it. Give students a chance to tell the story of a real-life trip or a portion of their spiritual journey. Or tell their story from your perspective. They love to hear us rejoice in their victories and realize that we understood the adversity they faced along the way. Make sure there is a discernible starting point; a summary of experiences and encounters; and a hopeful, open-ended finish that leaves room for great expectations in the future.

Tenth-of-a-Mile Formula

Just like the way I noticed the tenth-of-a-mile markers in Missouri, adolescents need us to notice their tenth-of-a-mile progress along the adolescent road. It means so much to them that we send a card, take them out for ice cream "just because," or even text them to wish them a fabulous first day at school.

A Youth Pastor's or Parent's Benediction

This is the poetic summary of truth. It's the personal prayer for God's continued enlightenment and transformation in a person's life. It's the challenge to go forward, live differently, and believe wholeheartedly. It's the reminder to take all that's been learned and gained and now live it. An original personal benediction written with a specific recipient in mind can tie a lot of lessons together and inspire a lot of future choices. Keep it simple, keep it short, but leave them wanting to reach high and go far. And as an added gift, give them a printed version to keep.

EXIT RAMP

Ring That Bell!

For almost five years, we exercised a small celebration in our student ministry office every time a project was completed. While John Lenschow was the fearless staff leader of our middle school ministry, a small service bell sat on top of the main office filing cabinet. When an event was a success, a task was completely wrapped up, or a ministry season finished, someone would walk through the office and ring the bell. Sometimes we even topped off the bell ring with a quick run for coffee at Starbucks. John taught us to stop at various intervals throughout the year and have a party. We were essentially taking a deep breath and briefly relaxing before the next endeavor got underway.

Looking all the way back to the years when my parents took in foster children, I've learned that, for the most part, adolescents experience a lot more oppression, aggression, depression, and criticism than celebration. So when they finish a portion of the journey or get through a remarkable storm or overcome tremendous obstacles—we need to throw joyous parties, highlight their victories with creativity, and say their names and accomplishments over and over again. We need to let them ring some bells and make some noise over the miles they've just traveled.

During my years at Redeemer, the grand finale was the Senior Banquet. We often heard from students and parents that out of all of the graduation parties and events their family attended, ours was the most meaningful. It wasn't because of extravagant decorations or expensive food and entertainment. Of course the room always looked beautiful and the food was excellent, but it was the ethos of celebration that captivated most in attendance. Our goal was that every student in the room would feel as though the entire party could have been thrown just for him or her alone.

It began with a huge senior picture display that went up in the church's welcome center three weeks earlier. Every week, hundreds of people would pass by and admire the handsome photos. At the actual party, the memory video included lots of growing-up pictures of everyone and fun interview segments to reminisce about their high school experience. The event's speaker wasn't a stranger giving a 30-minute canned graduation message. Instead, five or six influential adult leaders from our student ministry would share their specific hopes and prayers for that graduating class. When the students came forward to receive their senior gift, we read their names and left plenty of time for cheering and applause in between. (That little extra isn't allowed in most graduation ceremonies.) Through it all, we made sure they looked back and saw how far they'd come, and then I'd attempt to launch their hopes and dreams for adulthood with an original benediction written for their class.

Those were the very best days of ministry for me. They were bittersweet endings, but joyous beginnings, too. While greeting and hugging students after the conclusion of the organized party, or meeting them for coffee before they moved away to a new career after college, I'd begin another celebration. In those embraces, in those tears of gratefulness and friendship, I could sense—no, I knew–they were ready to go to a new place in their lives. They were high on the mountain, and through the help of so many people and experiences, God had led them through the incredible wilderness that now lay behind them.

1. Where do we need to do more celebrating with the adolescents in our lives?

2. What reminders could really encourage them and strengthen them?

3. What small places and intervals would be great for acknowledging the "one-tenth of a mile" idea?

4. Where can parents and youth workers partner more in celebrating and reminding?

BENEDICTION

Wherever you go,
May you encounter a young life
to lead down the road toward adulthood..

Whoever you are,
May you discover that it's within you to make a difference and
leave an imprint on the journey of one who is just beginning.

Whenever he needs a moment to grow, learn, or celebrate,
May you be right there alongside him,
enjoying the trip.

And…

Whatever you do,
May you travel the well-worn path of following Christ
and take a few young friends with you.

BIBLIOGRAPHY

Anderson, Cliff, and Dan Jessup. "Leadership in Youth Ministry." Course offered through Fuller Theological Seminary in Colorado Springs, CO,2005.

Bundschuh, Rick. *On Site: 40 On-Location Youth Programs.* Grand Rapids, MI: Zondervan/Youth Specialties, 1989.

Clark, Chap. "Youth Outreach and Evangelism." Course offered through Fuller Theological Seminary in Colorado Springs, CO, July 1998.

Fields, Doug, and Duffy Robbins. *Memory Makers: 50 Moments Your Kids Will Never Forget.* Grand Rapids, MI: Zondervan/Youth Specialties, 1996.

Hersch, Patricia. *A Tribe Apart: A Journey into the Heart of American Adolescence.* New York: Random House, 1999.

Meredith, Char. *It's a Sin to Bore a Kid: The Story of Young Life.* Waco, TX: Word Books, 1978.

Mueller, Walt. *Understanding Today's Youth Culture.* Wheaton, IL: Tyndale House, 1999.

Peterson, Eugene H. *The Jesus Way: A Conversation on the Ways that Jesus is the Way.* Grand Rapids, MI: Wm. B. Eerdmans Publishing Company, 2007.

Polich, Laurie. *Help! I'm a Small-Group Leader!* Grand Rapids, MI: Zondervan/Youth Specialties, 1998.

Polich, Laurie, and Charley Scandlyn. *Small Group Strategies: Ideas and Activities for Developing Spiritual Growth in Your Students.* Grand Rapids, MI: Zondervan/Youth Specialties, 2005.

Rayburn III, Jim. *From Bondage to Liberty, Dance, Children, Dance.* Colorado Springs, CO: Morningstar Press, 2000.

Steinbock, Steven E. *These Words Upon Our Heart: A Lexicon of Judaism and World Religions.* New York: UAHC Press, 2003.

Wangerin, Walter Jr. *Ragman: and Other Cries of Faith.* New York: HarperCollins, 2004.

ENDNOTES

1. Dr. Chap Clark, Youth Outreach and Evangelism Class. (Fuller Seminary, Colorado Springs, July 1998.) Used by permission.

2. Ibid.

3. Ibid.

4. Patricia Hersch, *A Tribe Apart: A Journey into the Heart of American Adolescence* (New York: Random House, 1998).

5. For more information, check out the Web site at www.davinciinstitute.com.

6. Christine Lagorio, "Resources: Marketing to Kids," CBS Evening News Web site, FYI Page, May 17, 2007, http://www.cbsnews.com/stories/2007/05/14/fyi/main2798401.shtml (accessed 4/4/09).

7. The Century Council, "Underage Drinking Fact Sheet," 2005, www.yellodyno.com/pdf/AlcDrg_Century_Council.pdf (accessed 4/5/09).

8. About.com: Christian Teens, QuickTips Index page, "Fun Bible Facts: By the Numbers," http://christianteens.about.com/od/understandingyourbible/qt/NumberFacts.htm (accessed 4/5/09).

9. Walter Wangerin, Jr., *Ragman: And Other Cries of Faith* (New York: HarperCollins, 2004).

10. http://en.wikipedia.org/wiki/1967_NFL_Draft and http://www.49ers.com/history/detail.php?year=1967 (accessed 4/7/09).

11. Jim Rayburn III, *From Bondage to Liberty, Dance, Children, Dance* (Colorado Springs, CO: Morningstar Press, 2000), Front Flap.

12. Rick Bundschuh, *On Site: 40 On-Location Youth Programs* (Grand Rapids, MI: Zondervan/Youth Specialties, 1989).

13. Eugene H. Peterson, *The Jesus Way: A Conversation on the Ways that Jesus Is the Way* (Grand Rapids, MI: Wm B. Eerdmans Publishing Company, 2007).

14. Doug Fields and Duffy Robbins, *Memory Makers: 50 Moments Your Kids Will Never Forget* (Grand Rapids, MI: Zondervan/Youth Specialties, 1996), 74–75.

15. Walter Wangerin, Jr., *Ragman: and Other Cries of Faith* (New York: HarperCollins, 2004).

16. Steven E. Steinbock, "N'shamah: The Breath of God, the Soul of the World Part 2," (adapted from his book *These Words Upon Our Heart),* posted October 30, 2007, http://www.nfty.org/Articles/index. cfm?id=7087&pge_prg_id=12041&pge_id=2481 (accessed 4/5/09).